To Patty,
Good luck and
enjoy the adventure!
Sandhya
12/08

Simple

Vegetarian

Cooking

With Spices that are easily available in Supermarkets

Most recipes suitable for Vegans

By

Sandy Ramesh

Recipe Photography: Ramesh Madhavan & Genie Lomba

Cover Design: Genie Lomba Photography

Interior Format & Design: Ramesh Madhavan

For questions, comments and details regarding permission, email to: Sandy.ramesh@cox.net

ISBN#: 1440415579

EAN-13: 9781440415579

Printed in United States of America.

First Edition: November 2008

Dedication

I dedicate this book to my father late Prof. P.D Mahadev and my mother Sharda.

Acknowledgements

I would like to thank Ms Kathy McQueeney for giving me the idea to write a cook book and Ms Bhaghyalakshmi of Mysore, India for guiding me in the right direction. Harry and Joyce Greenberg of Northern Connecticut Vegetarian Society [NCVS] opened the world of vegans to me and I thank them for expanding my horizons. Mrs. Uma Magge of South Windsor, CT has given me helpful hints and tips in cooking healthy food and I am very thankful for her advice.

My family has been very supportive of me in my ventures. My father introduced different cuisines and the art of fine dining to me. My mother being a good cook taught me not just cooking but also to be organized, meticulous and creative in my work habits. My husband Ramesh, daughters Deepta and Apoorva have endured all the tasting and testing of recipes. Further they provided all the technical help necessary to complete this book. I sincerely thank all of them for their patience and positive contributions. Further I would like to thank the manager and staff of Super Stop and Shop, South Windsor, Connecticut for their help.

CONTENTS

Recipe Index

Recipe Index (contd.)

Introduction

Before you put this book back on the bookstore shelf, let me assure you that this is not another Indian cookbook filled with exotic spices and complicated recipes. To avoid recipes that take an eternity to decipher, I have managed to simplify the recipes, used spices [McCormick] that are easily available in a standard American supermarket, and ensured that the overall process does not take too much of one's labor, time or patience. With this assurance I am confident that you will try out the recipes one by one. You will soon realize cooking with Indian spices is not difficult and perhaps may even make you improvise to suit your taste. I am not trying to promote vegetarianism but just sharing few recipes to create healthy and wholesome food.

I hold a Master's degree in Economics and a post graduate diploma in Environmental Planning. I did teach Economics for three years before getting married. Marriage changed the course of my life. I was able to see the world, live in different continents and experience amazing life. Being born and brought up in India this was an exciting experience. As I was brought up vegetarian, it was difficult to shop for food in a non English speaking country [Switzerland]. It was here that I realized that good Indian food can be cooked even in the absence of 'essential' ingredients. Substitutes are always available and one must learn as how to use them. When I came to USA, I had all the ingredients available in an Indian grocery store but did not have daily domestic help unlike India. With two children it was difficult to manage the house; hence I had to depend on appliances and gadgets to get work done. As adaptability has been my strong point, I feel confident about my recipes which are simple [most of them] yet delicious.

I cooked everyday as I had no other alternative. Though I did enjoy cooking in my younger days, it was now becoming a chore. So I started becoming creative by simplifying yet not compromising on taste. This made me very interested in cooking once again and my family and friends were appreciative of my culinary talent [may be they were being polite]. The moment I started enjoying cooking which is in reality an art by itself, I was helping/guiding family and friends with hints and tips. Likewise I was always eager to learn new recipes and techniques too. I did prepare a recipe book for my own use but never imagined publishing one.

A chance meeting with a lady [I later came to know her name was Kathy] at a yoga studio, made me think otherwise. Kathy asked me whether I was Indian and could I teach her few simple recipes. I agreed and she came next day and I prepared a simple but wholesome meal which she really enjoyed. She found that Indian cooking was not intimidating and encouraged me to write a cook book. I went to a book store and found plenty of Indian cook books which are very good, but most have plenty of non-vegetarian recipes. Next, the ingredients are too many [some unheard of] and the procedure lengthy and complicated. The recipes written are wonderful if you are Indian.

Then I visited our local supermarket to see the availability of ingredients. McCormick has a wonderful range of spices and I have used only those spices available in the McCormick brand. Further I have used vegetables, beans, peas, rice etc which are available in American supermarket.

Indian food is generally associated with spices, oil and watery eyes. Indians have a love affair with spices, red chilli powder, oil, cilantro leaves and other herbs. When I cook I am able to use less spices, salt and oil, yet create a tasty dish which is friendly to the stomach too. Indian cooking is based on the science of 'ayurveda' which in Sanskrit means 'knowledge of life'. The science of ayurveda uses spices, minerals, oil, herbs and animal by products to heal and cure ailments. Spices like cumin, pepper, ginger, asafoetida and fenugreek seeds helps in relieving discomfort in the digestive system. Fenugreek seeds have known to lower blood sugar levels. Spices like mustard seeds, fennel seeds, pepper, cardamom, saffron, turmeric powder etc are used in daily cooking not just for flavor but for medicinal benefits too.

Spices have played an important role in history. Arabs had the monopoly of spice trade by bringing the spices from the east [India, China etc] and selling it to Europeans. The land route to India via the Khyber Pass was not safe for European merchants. Hence the desire to find a sea route to India and the east led to the adventures of Vasco da Gama and Christopher Columbus. In 1498 AD Vasco da Gama landed in Calicut, which is in the state of Kerala, India. The state of Kerala which is in south west of the country is extremely rich in pepper, cloves, cinnamon, cardamom and other spices. Thus the Portuguese established trade relations with India and spices found their way easily into the European kitchens. Today we use spices in drinks, dinners and desserts. In India we have been using spices on a daily basis from time immemorial.

I was not very familiar or clear about the concept of vegans. After I attended a meeting of Northern Connecticut Vegetarian Society [NCVS] and understood the philosophy of vegans, I realized that Indian cooking is almost vegan friendly. It is true that as a nation we are obsessed with dairy products, but we have rules akin to 'kosher' where we cannot mix grains or cooked vegetables with milk or yogurt [certain exceptions do exist]. The logic behind this concept is scientific. India being hot and humid most of the time, certain rules were made to protect the food from spoiling. Milk does spoil very soon and cow being sacred to us Hindus, efforts were made to see that milk which is auspicious doesn't split. The wise men of ancient times were very rational, logical and scientific in their thought.

This made me think that most of the recipes are vegan friendly. I have few recipes that have yogurt or milk as the main ingredient and those recipes have been clearly marked as 'not suitable for vegans'. But most of the recipes are suitable for vegans. I sincerely hope vegans find these recipes useful.

Further I have used very less oil/butter in the recipes to make it healthier. I use canola oil in cooking but you can use whichever oil you are comfortable with. No doubt rich food tastes very good, but it is not healthy physically or mentally. Rich food tends to make one sluggish, drowsy and inactive, but having a little ghee which is the Indian word for clarified butter does enhance the taste of the food. Ghee is very greasy and it may take a while to get used to it. Ghee is generally used for applying on rotis as it makes it soft and aromatic. To make ghee, place a stick of butter in a saucepan and heat it over medium heat. After a couple of minutes you will see the butter melting and a white residue floating.

When the molten butter turns to a golden yellow transparent liquid and white residue turns brown, remove from heat and let it cool awhile. Strain the molten butter into a bottle and throw out the brown residue. If you live in cooler climate, the liquid will solidify into a pleasant yellow ghee.

This is a substitute for oil and can be used in rotis, sweetened cream of wheat, vegetable pilaf to name a few. In case you use, please use very little so as to not block the arteries in the heart. Being diabetic I have to keep myself active, so I workout in the gym for an hour and follow it with an hour of yoga every day. In summer I try to swim ½ mile daily, weather permitting. After such an active day, I prefer to eat more of vegetables, beans, peas and less of rice.

There are some aspects where I am unable to give exact measurement. Salt is an essential ingredient but each person has their own way of salting their food. A grain of salt less is preferable to a grain of salt more. Please bear in mind that the quantity of vegetables when cooked does reduce, sometimes considerably. It is advisable to add little salt, taste and then add more if required. Further it is not possible to estimate the exact amount of water as these depend on lot of variables, hence use your own judgment. Fresh food does taste very good, try to cook in such a way that you have less leftovers.

Please feel free to use your own imagination and creativity to improvise any recipe. After all, I have just given the basic guideline; customize to suit your palate. There is no right or wrong in cooking.

A clean and organized kitchen makes cooking an enjoyable activity. Always clear away the unwanted clutter from the counter and have a clean sink, this simple act works wonder. I try to cook with a calm frame of mind and I have noticed that the mood is directly proportional to quality of output. But frankly speaking it is almost impossible to cook calmly and in an organized manner on a daily basis. I do try my best.

Having certain pots pan and gadgets does make life easier. One such example is a pressure cooker. All Indian households have minimum of one pressure cooker at least. This speeds up cooking beans, peas, lentils, rice and certain vegetables. If you plan on eating rice regularly, investing in a rice cooker is worth it.

Similarly if you have lot of chopping, grating etc [like me] a food processor is a good investment. As my recipes involve lot of seasoning, buying a small pan [like a one egg wonder from T-FAL as shown below] is appropriate. The rest of the cookware like skillets, saucepans, ladles, griddles is always there in any kitchen.

Spices don't come cheap and keeping spices for too long in the pantry results in loss of flavor. To avoid wastage please buy small bottles of spices. I have used only few spices so that you can mix and match them. This way you do not have too many bottles sitting on the spice rack.

As I had to modify the recipes from the original, I have tried each recipe at least few times before writing it down. My style of seasoning is different from what you are used to, try it a couple of times and you will master it. Use a splatter screen when you add the mustard seeds. It is advisable to keep the seasoning ready even before the oil heats up.

Please do not feel disheartened when a recipe does not turn out the way it is supposed to be. Do not throw it unless it is burnt. Walk out of the kitchen and after the frustration and disappointment washes away, go back into the kitchen and figure out how to make it edible with a calm mind, you will surely come up with some idea.

Many a times the cook books we buy are proudly displayed on a shelf in the kitchen but rarely used. This book is not for display, but for regular use. So if it gets dirty, oily and stained with regular wear and tear, it will be my most satisfying moment as it indicates 'friendliness' of the book. Open the book and let the adventures begin.

Basic Shopping List

Whole Spices/Seasonings

1. Mustard seeds
2. Yellow split peas
3. Cumin seeds
4. Fennel seeds
5. Red chillies
6. Turmeric powder
7. Red chilli powder
8. Garam masala powder
9. Curry powder
10. Cumin powder
11. Ground coriander

Herbs etc.

1. Cilantro leaves
2. Mint leaves
3. Jalapeno pepper
4. Ginger
5. Garlic

The Essential Spices

GROUND Turmeric

Chili Powder

YELLOW Mustard SEED

Cumin SEED

Fennel SEED

Curry Powder

GROUND Cumin

GARAM MASALA

GROUND CORIANDER SEED

Vegetables-Nature's Bounty

One of the definitions for the word "vegetable" according to Webster's New World College Dictionary is "any herbaceous plant that is eaten whole or in part, raw or cooked". For me the word vegetable means one of the amazing creations on Earth which is not just nutritious but delicious too. The sight of fresh grown vegetables is certainly very appetizing and it does bring out the hidden creativity in many of us.

At times I do feel I have a healthy obsession for fresh produce and it dates back to 1980's when I was in my teens. I was born and brought up in India and we had a nice yard and most importantly a gardener. Somehow my family assigned me the duty to supervise the gardener and get the work done. I took an active interest in flower beds, potted plants, light landscaping, etc. We had a large backyard and it was decided to make it into a vegetable garden. Also, cheap labor makes many things possible. When the monsoon season arrived [mid June], we would plant green beans, okras, eggplants, tomatoes, chayote squash, bitter melon, green chilies, cilantro, spinach, fenugreek leaves, mint, etc.

There were already fruit bearing trees like mango, papaya, pomegranate, guavas, banana, gooseberry and coconut.

Further our town horticulture office supplied saplings of fruit, vegetable and flower plants and also advised us in these matters to encourage horticulture. Thus we had a beautiful and bountiful garden and the tropical weather helped us to do so.

After school I would walk around our back yard to take stock of vegetables that were ready to be picked. Depending on availability of vegetables, my mother would plan the next day's menu. We did not depend on our garden entirely, but on the days we cooked our own home grown vegetables, it was indeed very satisfying. The gardener was well rewarded with generous home cooked food [apart from his pay] and it was around this time I really started to appreciate 'the nature's bounty'.

Times changed and so did me, but my love for vegetables did not diminish. I spent a lot of time with my studies and later with my teaching job. I got married, preferred to stay home and thus began my complete involvement with the kitchen. I tried experimenting by creating new recipes; some experiments did work well, while many did not.

In 1993 we spent four months in Zurich, Switzerland.

It was an eye opener as I saw vegetables like lettuce, celery, broccoli, parsley, peppers of various hues and other vegetables. Though I had seen pictures of these, I had not seen them as they were not available in India in those days [before globalization process]. Being clueless as to how to cook them, language being a barrier, no family or friends to guide me, I spent the winter afternoons trying to prepare something edible in our Spartan kitchen with little or no access to Indian condiments. Either the spices were not available or they were too expensive for us to afford.

This experience made me learn to live with what is available and to modify the traditional recipes. In 1996 we moved to Barbados, by then we had two daughters and again the experience in this Caribbean country was very pleasant and enjoyable. The equatorial climate brought forth the abundance of fresh produce and I started incorporating the available vegetables in our day to day life.

In 1998 we moved once again and this time to Connecticut, USA. I had the best of both the worlds and cooking became a joy as I had honed my culinary skills by then. The Indian grocery stores took care of all our ethnic needs while the American supermarkets had wide array of produce. It was in this country that I learned to incorporate the east and the west worlds and create simple yet delicious recipes with Indian spices.

The recipes in the following pages are very simple. Some may appear to be a bit lengthy or complicated, but it is not so. I have deliberately refrained from using too many ingredients to be user friendly. Most importantly I have used only the produce and spices available in an American supermarket. Some might feel it is not so authentic, but my aim is to help people cook Indian food without the hassle to searching for an Indian grocery store to buy the ingredients. In this age and time it is very important to keep things simple and not slave away in the kitchen on everyday basis.

Word of caution: Please use your own judgment while using oil, spices, salt and water. Though the recipes provide a guideline, you may want to alter to suit your taste. Cooking is after all custom- made to suit your own preference. Care must be taken while adding salt as the quantity of raw vegetables decrease, sometimes significantly after cooking.

I do hope you will find the following vegetable recipes easy to make and nourishing too. To make the dishes attractive, I have a tendency to mix two colors, but go ahead and have fun trying out these recipes and making changes to suit your palate when required.

1. Beets
(Suitable for Vegans)
<u>SERVES 2-3</u>

Ingredients

1 large beet, peeled and chopped
1 medium sized potato, chopped
1 large carrot, chopped

Seasonings

¾ tsp mustard seeds
1 tsp yellow split peas
1" long dried red chilli
A dash of turmeric powder
2 tsp of oil
2 tsp of finely chopped cilantro leaves
Salt

Method

Cook the beets, carrots and potatoes separately. Drain any excess water and keep aside. Heat oil in a skillet and before it smokes add the mustard seeds, yellow split peas, dried red chilli and turmeric powder. Cover and when mustard seeds stop spluttering, add the beets, carrots and potatoes. Add salt and mix well. Discard the red chilli and sprinkle the cilantro leaves before serving. This dish can be served hot or warm.

Note: This preparation can be served with rice or can be eaten with Indian flat bread or tortilla. If fresh grated coconut is available, sprinkle 2 tsp of it before serving. Store unused portion in refrigerator and reheat well before serving.

2. Cabbage
(Suitable for Vegans)
SERVES 2-3

Ingredients

3 cups of finely chopped cabbage
¼ cup green peas [frozen or fresh]

Seasonings

¾ tsp mustard seeds
1 tsp yellow split peas
1"long dried red chilli
A dash of turmeric powder
A dash of ginger powder
Salt
2 tsp oil

Microwave Method

Place cabbage in a microwave safe bowl. Heat oil in a small pan and before it smokes add the mustard seeds, yellow split peas, dried red chilli, turmeric powder and ginger powder. Cover. When mustard seeds stop spluttering, pour this seasoning over the cabbage, add salt, mix well, cover and microwave on high for about 3 minutes. Now mix in peas and microwave for another minute. Discard the chilli before serving.

Stovetop Method

Heat oil in a skillet and before it smokes add the mustard seeds, yellow split peas, dried red chilli, turmeric powder and ginger powder. Cover and once the mustard seeds stop spluttering add the cabbage, sprinkle little water, cover and cook on low medium heat. After about 5 minutes add the peas, salt, mix well and cook till done. Discard the chilli before serving. This preparation can be served hot or warm.

> **Note:** This preparation can be enjoyed with rice or flat bread. The ginger powder is added to relieve the discomfort some people experience after eating cabbage. If fresh grated coconut is available, add 2 tsp of it before serving. Kindly refrigerate any unused portion and reheat well before serving.

3. Carrots
(Suitable for Vegans)
<u>SERVES 2-3</u>

Ingredients

4 large carrots, peeled/well scrubbed, chopped
¼ cup green peas [frozen or fresh]

Seasonings

¾ tsp mustard seeds
1 tsp yellow split peas
1"long dried red chilli
A dash of turmeric powder
2 tsp oil
2 tsp finely chopped cilantro leaves
Salt

Microwave Method

Place the chopped carrots in a microwave safe bowl. Heat oil in a small pan and before it smokes add the mustard seeds, yellow split peas, dried chilli and turmeric powder. Cover and when the mustard seeds stop spluttering, pour this seasoning over the carrots, add salt, mix well. Cover and microwave on high for about 3 minutes. Now add the peas, mix well and microwave for about a minute. Discard the chilli and sprinkle the cilantro leaves before serving.

Stovetop Method

Heat oil in a skillet and before it smokes add the mustard seeds, yellow split peas, dried chilli and turmeric powder. Cover, and when the mustard seeds stop spluttering, add the carrots, sprinkle little water and cook covered for 4 to 5 minutes. Now add the peas and salt, mix well and cook covered for another minute. Add little water to avoid burning. When done, discard the chilli, sprinkle the cilantro leaves. Serve it hot or warm.

Note: Please use you own judgment while adding water, and see to it that there is no excess water after the carrots are cooked. This preparation can be served with rice or flat bread. If available add 2 tsp of fresh grated coconut just before serving, not only does it enhance the taste but the appearance too. Store unused portion if any in refrigerator and reheat well before serving.

Cauliflower in gravy

4. Cauliflower in Gravy
(Suitable for Vegans)
SERVES 3

Ingredients

3 cups of cauliflower florets
1 medium size potato, cubed
1 medium size tomato, diced
¼ cup green peas
1 small onion thinly sliced
1 cup water

Seasonings

½ tsp cumin seeds
½ tsp fennel seeds
1 tsp garam masala
¼ tsp turmeric powder
¼ tsp red chilli powder
2 tsp oil
2 tsp finely chopped cilantro leaves
Salt

Method

Heat oil in a skillet and before it smokes add the cumin and fennel seeds. Once the seeds brown, add the onions and sauté for about 2-3 minutes. Now add the tomatoes, turmeric powder, red chilli powder and garam masala. Cook for about 2 minutes. Add the potatoes, cauliflower florets, peas and salt. Mix well and add little water and cook covered on low medium heat till potatoes are done. Turn once in 5 minutes to avoid burning and for uniform cooking. Garnish with cilantro leaves before serving. This curry tastes very good when served hot.

Note: Kindly use your own judgment while adding water as there is a little gravy in this preparation. For better appearance microwave the peas in little water for a minute and add it to the skillet before removing from heat. The peas retain a brilliant green color and make the preparation look attractive. Serve it with rice or flat bread. Store unused portion in the refrigerator and reheat well before serving.

5. Cauliflower- Simple
(Suitable for Vegans)
<u>SERVES 2 -3</u>

Ingredients

3 cups of cauliflower florets
1 medium sized tomato chopped
1 small onion thinly sliced

Seasonings

½ tsp cumin seeds
1 tsp curry powder
Less than ¼ tsp turmeric powder
¼ tsp red chilli powder
3 tsp of oil
2 tsp of finely chopped cilantro
leaves
Salt
½ cup water [approximately]

Method

Heat oil in a skillet and before it smokes add the cumin seeds and let it brown slightly. Now add the onions and sauté for 2-3 minutes. When onions are slightly brown add the tomatoes, turmeric powder, curry powder and chilli powder. Sauté for a minute, and then add the cauliflower florets, salt and sprinkle little water. Cook covered on low medium heat. Turn the vegetables about once in 5 minutes to avoid burning and for uniform cooking. When cauliflower turns soft, the dish is ready to be served. Sprinkle cilantro leaves just before serving. This preparation tastes good when served hot.

Note: Microwave the cauliflower florets for about 2 minutes and then add it to the skillet. This fastens the cooking process, but do not overcook the florets. This preparation tastes delicious with rice, flat bread, tortillas, bread, bun and bagels. Store unused portion in the refrigerator and reheat well before serving.

6. Egg Plant
(Suitable for Vegans)
<u>SERVES 3</u>

Ingredients

1 eggplant cubed
1 medium size potato cubed
1 medium size tomato diced
1 small onion thinly sliced

Seasonings

½ tsp mustard seeds
½ tsp cumin seeds
1 tsp curry powder
¼ tsp chilli powder
Less than ¼ tsp turmeric powder
3 tsp oil
2 tsp finely chopped cilantro leaves
Salt

Method

Heat oil in a skillet and before it smokes add the mustard seeds and the cumin seeds. When the mustard seeds stop popping, add the onions and sauté for about 2 minutes. Now add the eggplant, potatoes, tomatoes, curry powder, chilli powder, turmeric powder and salt. Mix well and cook covered on low medium heat. Turn often to avoid burning and for uniform cooking. Garnish with the cilantro leaves before serving. Serve hot.

Note: Four tsp of coarsely powdered roasted peanuts can be added just before removing the skillet from heat. This preparation is very delicious and can be served with rice, flat breads or just warm bread of any kind. Store any unused portion in the refrigerator and reheat well before serving.

7. Broiled Egg Plant
(Suitable for Vegans)
SERVES 2-3

Ingredients

1 large eggplant
1 medium size onion finely chopped
1 tomato diced
¼ cup green peas

Seasonings

1 tsp cumin seeds
¼ tsp chilli powder
Less than ¼ tsp turmeric powder
Less than ¼ tsp ginger powder or 1 tsp grated ginger
¼ tsp garlic powder or 1 flake of garlic chopped
½ tsp garam masala
4 tsp oil
2 tsp finely chopped cilantro leaves
Salt

Method

Apply a tsp of oil to the eggplant, wrap it in aluminum foil and broil for around 45 minutes, turning it halfway around after 30 minutes. When the eggplant is well done, cool it, peel it and mash it into a pulp. Keep aside.

Heat oil in a skillet and add the cumin seeds. When the cumin seeds brown, add the onions and sauté it for 2-3 minutes. Now add the tomatoes, peas, turmeric powder, chilli powder, garam masala, garlic and ginger and cook for about 3 minutes. Now add the eggplant pulp and salt, mix well and cook for about 5-7 minutes on low medium heat, stirring often. Garnish with cilantro leaves before serving. Serve hot.

Note: The recipe may appear complicated but it is not so. Enjoy this preparation with rice, flat bread or any kind of warm bread. Store any unused portion in the refrigerator and reheat well before serving.

8. Green Beans
(Suitable for Vegans)
SERVES 2

Ingredients

2 cups of green beans, cut into small pieces
¼ cup carrots cut into small pieces

Seasonings

½ tsp mustard seeds
1 tsp yellow split peas
1"long dried red chilli
1-2 tsp of oil
Salt

Microwave method

Place the green beans and the carrots in a microwave safe bowl. Heat oil in a small pan and before it smokes add the mustard seeds, split peas and dried chilli. Cover. When the mustard seeds stop popping, pour this seasoning on green beans and carrots. Add salt, mix well and microwave on high in the covered bowl for 2 minutes. Stir once and microwave again for 2 minutes or till cooked. Discard the chilli before serving.

Stovetop cooking

Steam the green beans and carrots till tender. Keep aside. Heat oil in a skillet and before it smokes add the mustard seeds, yellow split peas and the dried red chilli. Cover. When the mustard seeds stop popping, reduce heat, add the beans and carrots, salt and mix well. Cook for about 2-3 minutes. Discard the chilli before serving.

> Note: if available sprinkle 2 tsp of fresh grated coconut before serving. Serve it as a side dish to any rice preparation. Please store any unused portion in the refrigerator and reheat well before serving.

Mixed vegetable stir-fry

9. Mixed Vegetable Stir-Fry
(Suitable for Vegans)
SERVES 3

Ingredients

1 lb of mixed vegetables [green beans, carrots, cauliflower, peppers, broccoli, potato, sweet corn, green peas, lima beans, etc]
1 small onion finely sliced

Seasonings

1 tsp cumin seeds
1/2 tsp fennel seeds
1 tsp curry powder
Less than 1/4 tsp red chilli powder
1 tsp grated ginger or less than ¼ tsp ginger powder
2 tsp oil
Salt
2 tsp cilantro leaves finely chopped

Method

Cut green beans, carrots, cabbage, peppers, and potatoes into long pieces. Heat oil in a skillet and before it smokes add the cumin seeds and the fennel seeds. Let it brown slightly. Now add the onions and sauté for about 2 to 3 minutes. Now add all the vegetables, curry powder, red chilli powder, ginger, and salt. Mix well. Add little water and cook covered on low medium heat. Stir often to avoid burning and for uniform cooking and taste. Once the potatoes are cooked, remove from heat. Other vegetables can remain slightly crunchy. Garnish with cilantro leaves before serving.

Note: this is an excellent preparation with the leftover vegetables in the refrigerator. If you are using broccoli florets, microwave them for a minute and add it skillet after the heat is turned off. Please store any unused portion in the refrigerator and reheat well before serving.

10. Okra
(Suitable for Vegans)
SERVES 2-3

Ingredients

1 lb okra, washed, dried and cut into ½" discs
1 small onion finely sliced
1 small potato cubed
1 small tomato diced

Seasonings

½ tsp cumin seeds
½ tsp fennel seeds
Less than ¼ tsp turmeric powder
¼ tsp red chilli powder
½ tsp garam masala
4 tsp oil
Salt
2 tsp of finely chopped cilantro leaves

Method

Place the okras on a microwave safe plate lined with paper towel. Microwave for a minute or two. This helps to remove the sliminess in the okras and also helps in faster cooking. Keep aside. Heat oil in a skillet and add the cumin and fennel seeds. When they brown, add the onions and sauté for about 2 minutes. Now add the okras, potatoes, tomatoes, turmeric powder, chilli powder, garam masala and salt. Mix well, cover and cook on low medium heat. After about 10 minutes mix well and cook uncovered till okras are done. Keep stirring often to avoid burning. Sprinkle cilantro leaves before serving. Serve hot.

Alternate method

Preheat oven to 350 degrees Fahrenheit. Line a baking dish with aluminum foil. After adding the vegetables and spices to the skillet, mix well and transfer the entire contents to the baking dish. Cover with aluminum foil and bake for about 10 minutes. Mix well and then bake uncovered till okras are done. Sprinkle cilantro leaves before serving. Serve hot.

Note: Cooking in a skillet will require constant attention, while baking in an oven will result in higher electric or gas consumption. The okras will reduce in quantity considerably after cooking.

Okras are an all time favorite with most Indians, but people in this country are not very familiar with this vegetable. Don't be hesitant to try it, after all life is full of experiments and new experiences. This preparation tastes extremely delicious when served with hot Indian flat bread. Good luck!! Kindly refrigerate any unused portion and reheat well before serving.

11. Peppers
(Suitable for Vegans)
<u>SERVES 2</u>

Ingredients

1 large green pepper cut into long pieces
1 large red pepper cut into long pieces
1 small onion thinly sliced
1 medium potato cut into long pieces [like French fry cut]

Seasonings

½ tsp cumin seeds
¼ tsp ground coriander
Less than ¼ tsp turmeric powder
Less than ¼ tsp red chilli powder
¼ tsp curry powder
2 tsp oil
Salt

Method

Heat oil in a skillet and before it smokes add the cumin seeds. After a minute add the onions and sauté for 2 minutes. Now add the potatoes and let it cook for 2 minutes. Add the peppers, turmeric powder, chilli powder, ground coriander, curry powder and salt. Mix well and cook uncovered on low medium heat till potatoes are done. Peppers can remain slightly crunchy. Serve hot.

Note: Use whatever peppers are on hand, I have mentioned 2 colors to make the dish look appealing. Do not overcook the peppers. Serve hot with flat breads, rice or any kind of warm bread. Store unused portion in the refrigerator and reheat well before serving.

Potatoes are a universal favorite. Culinary styles all over the world have exclusive recipes involving potatoes. Potatoes are cooked in various ways and sometimes in Indian cooking we add potatoes to absorb extra moisture to give the right consistency to the dish. At times it is added when a preparation becomes too salty, potatoes absorb the salt and make it palatable. Though I do use potatoes in cooking, I try to do it sparingly as I am diabetic. The use of spices in cooking potatoes helps in relieving the discomfort some may experience after eating potatoes.

In the following pages I have mentioned some basic recipes using potatoes as the main ingredient. Hope you will have fun trying out these simple basic preparations.

12. *Mashed Potatoes*
(Suitable for Vegans)
<u>SERVES 2-3</u>

Ingredients

1 lb potatoes
1 small onion thinly sliced

Seasonings

½ tsp mustard seeds
½ tsp cumin seeds
1 tsp yellow split peas
1 small jalapeno pepper slit lengthwise
Less than ¼ tsp ginger powder or 1 tsp
   fresh grated ginger
Less than ¼ tsp turmeric powder
2 tsp oil
2 tsp finely chopped cilantro leaves
Salt
¼ to ½ water [if required]
A dash of lime juice [optional]

Method

Boil potatoes in salt water, peel and mash it coarsely using fingers or a potato masher. Do not mash it to smooth paste. Keep aside. Heat oil in a skillet and before it smokes add the mustard seeds, cumin seeds and yellow split peas. When the mustard seeds stop popping, add the jalapeno pepper, turmeric powder, ginger and onions. Sauté for 2 minutes, add the coarsely mashed potatoes and salt. Mix well with a light hand and cook for 3-4 minutes on low medium heat. Sprinkle little water if the dish becomes too dry. Discard the jalapeno pepper, garnish with lime juice and cilantro leaves before serving. Serve hot.

Note: Cumin seeds and ginger are used in this preparation not just to enhance the taste but for their medicinal value too. These 2 spices help in alleviating the discomfort some feel in their stomach after eating potatoes. This simple recipe can be enjoyed with any flat bread, as a patty for burgers or in grilled sandwiches. Please refrigerate any leftover portions and reheat well before serving.

13. Potatoes Fried
(Suitable for Vegans)
SERVES 2-3

Ingredients

1 lb potatoes cut into 2" long pieces
   [French fry cut]

Seasonings

1 tsp cumin seeds
Less than ¼ tsp turmeric powder
A dash or two of black pepper powder
4 tsp oil
Salt

Method

Heat oil in a skillet and before it smokes add the cumin seeds. When the cumin seeds brown, add turmeric powder to the oil and then add the potatoes. Reduce heat to low medium, mix well and cook covered for about 5 minutes. Now uncover, add salt and pepper powder, mix well and continue to cook uncovered till potatoes are well done. Serve hot.

Note: This preparation can be served with flat bread, any other kind of bread or rice. A dash or two of red chilli powder can be substituted for black pepper powder. Please store any unused portion in the refrigerator.

Potatoes in gravy

14. Potatoes in Gravy
(Suitable for Vegans)
<u>SERVES 2-3</u>

Ingredients

1 lb potatoes
1 medium size onion finely sliced
1 large tomato diced
1/3 cup green peas
1-2 cups water [as needed]

Seasonings

¾ tsp mustard seeds
1 tsp cumin seeds
½ tsp fennel seeds
1 tsp garam masala
¼ tsp red chilli powder
Less than ¼ tsp turmeric powder
Less than ¼ tsp ginger powder or 1 tsp fresh grated ginger
2 tsp oil
2 tsp finely chopped cilantro leaves
Salt

Method

Boil the potatoes in salt water, peel and cut them into cubes. Keep aside. Heat oil in a skillet and before it smokes, add the mustard seeds, cumin and fennel seeds. Once the mustard seeds stop popping add onions and sauté for 2 minutes, now add the tomatoes, turmeric powder, ginger powder, garam masala and red chilli powder. Add ½ cup of water and let the tomatoes cook for 3-4 minutes. Now add the potatoes, peas, salt and about 1 cup water, mix well and cook covered for about 5 minutes. Stir often for uniform taste. Sprinkle cilantro leaves before serving. Serve hot.

Note: This dish tastes excellent when served with hot Indian flat breads. Refrigerator any leftovers and reheat well before serving.

15. Simple Potatoes
(Suitable for Vegans)
<u>SERVES 2-3</u>

Ingredients

  1 lb potatoes

Seasonings

  ½ tsp mustard seeds
  Less than ¼ tsp turmeric powder
  ¼ tsp red chilli powder
  ½ tsp cumin powder
  2 tsp oil
  Salt

Method

Boil potatoes in salt water, peel and cut into cubes. Keep aside. Heat oil in a skillet and before it smokes add the mustard seeds. When mustard seeds stop popping, reduce heat, and add turmeric powder, chilli powder and cumin powder. Now add the cubed potatoes and salt. Mix well using a light hand till the spices uniformly coats the potatoes. Serve hot.

Note: Serve these potatoes with flat bread or on any kind of bread. Store the leftovers in the refrigerator.

Option- In case you are cooking in large quantity, transfer the potatoes from the skillet to a baking dish and bake them in the oven for 20 minutes at 350 degrees Fahrenheit for crispy potatoes. Sprinkle the cilantro leaves just before serving.

---

16. Seasoned Sweet Corn
(Suitable for Vegans)
SERVES 2

Ingredients

1 cup sweet corn kernels

Seasonings

½ tsp cumin powder
A dash or two of black pepper powder
Salt
1 tsp oil
A dash of lime juice
1 tsp cilantro leaves finely chopped

Method

Heat oil in a pan and before it smokes add cumin powder and the corn kernels. Mix well. Now add the pepper powder and salt, and cook covered on low medium heat. Sprinkle little water if required. When done add the lime juice and cilantro leaves. Enjoy this snack anytime.

Note: Store any unused portion in the refrigerator and reheat well before serving.

17. Spinach
(Suitable for Vegans)
SERVES 3

Ingredients

1 lb spinach, washed and chopped
1 small onion finely sliced
1 medium size potato cubed

Seasonings

½ tsp cumin seeds
¼ tsp fennel seeds
Less than ¼ tsp ginger powder or
1 tsp fresh grated ginger
Less than ¼ tsp turmeric powder
Less than ¼ tsp red chilli powder
½ tsp garam masala
2 tsp oil
1 cup water [approximately]
Salt

Method

Heat oil in a skillet and before it smokes add the cumin and fennel seeds. Once they brown add the ginger and onions and sauté for 2-3 minutes. Now add spinach, potatoes, turmeric powder, red chilli powder, garam masala and salt. Mix well, sprinkle little water and cook covered. Serve hot.

Note: It is your choice to use fresh or frozen spinach depending on availability and convenience. Serve this dish with flat bread or with rice. Please store any unused portion in the refrigerator.

18. Spinach with Tofu
(Suitable for Vegans)
SERVES 4

Ingredients

1 lb of spinach, washed and chopped
1 small onion finely chopped
1 medium size tomato diced
¼ cup peas
½ cup chopped carrots
1 cup tofu cubes [directions given below]

Seasonings

1 tsp cumin seeds
1 tsp curry powder
Less than ¼ tsp garlic powder or 1 flake of garlic chopped
¼ tsp red chilli powder
Less than ¼ tsp turmeric powder
2 tsp oil
½ to 1 cup water
Salt

Preparation of tofu cubes

Cut firm tofu into slices [like bread slices]. Place these slices on a hot flat griddle and brown them on both the sides. Cool it and cut into cubes. This process ensures that tofu cubes retain their shape during cooking. Store them in freezer and before using these cubes in curries, salads etc, thaw them on the counter or microwave them for a minute.

Method

Heat oil in a skillet and before it smokes add the cumin seeds. After a minute add the garlic and onions. Sauté for about 2 minutes. Now add the spinach, carrots, peas, tomato, tofu cubes, turmeric powder, red chilli powder, curry powder, salt and little water. Mix well and cook covered on low medium heat. Serve hot.

Note: In Indian cuisine, spinach with cottage cheese [paneer] is a very popular dish. But as paneer is not available in an American supermarket and is not suitable for vegans, I have used tofu instead. By trial and error method I figured out the best way to include tofu instead of paneer and glad to say I achieved what I intended to do. The flavors of the spices get infused into the tofu in the process of cooking and hence taste delicious. Serve this dish with flat bread, rice or enjoy a bowl as a snack.

Introduction

Webster's New World College Dictionary defines rice as 'the starchy seeds or grains of an aquatic cereal grass grown widely in warm climates, especially east Asia.'

For last 5000 years rice has been cultivated and consumed. In India it is a major food crop and it is prepared in different ways depending on geographical regions. Rice is the staple diet for people in south and eastern part of India, whereas in north and western India people eat more of wheat and less of rice. Growing up in southern India I was used to eating rice on a daily basis. We ate plain cooked rice with curries, seasoned with spices, cooked with vegetables, cooked with lentils and so on. Rice was made into flour or ground to a paste and prepared as flat bread, crepes, steamed cakes, crispy snacks etc. Further we had delicious dishes prepared out of puffed rice and beaten rice. An auspicious offering to Gods was dessert made with rice, milk and sugar. The possibilities are almost endless.

While growing up I was lucky to have fruit trees in our yard.   My mother prepared exotic delicacies like coconut rice, mango rice, pomegranate rice, gooseberry rice to add variety to our food. Further she was able to use the available produce on hand. During weddings and religious festivities [we had lots of these occasions] we use to over eat and then suffer immense discomfort. My grandmother who lived with us was very experienced and wise, made simple rice dishes using dill, basil, mint, broad thyme and spices.

These rice preparations were tasty and easy to digest. Amazing as it may sound, we recovered miraculously without medication.   The combination of spices and herbs she used was based on the science of ayurveda- the ancient Hindu system of using herbs, spices and oils to cure ailments. Though I was young, I was able to appreciate the value of this traditional science and experience the healing powers that lay in humble inexpensive spices and herbs which were in the pantry.

Now that I have diabetes, my intake of rice has been drastically reduced, but my enthusiasm has not. I still prepare a variety of rice dishes for my family and friends. In the following pages I have recipes which are simple to make.   Though I prepare many kinds of rice dishes, I have not included them as they are high labor intensive and need lots of ingredients which cannot be bought in an American supermarket. My aim is to keep things simple and hope I have done so.

Some recipes may appear complicated, but please don't be discouraged. Read the recipe couple of times and I am sure you will get the feel of it and figure out how to do it. Though there are different kinds of rice grains [long grained, jasmine, basmati, par boiled, brown, and organic, etc], I have used mostly basmati rice as it is non sticky and hence suitable for the recipes I have written. Please use the kind of rice you are comfortable with, I have merely suggested what I use when I prepare these rice varieties. Have a good time trying out the new rice dishes and you will be amazed at the results.

1. Plain Rice
(Suitable for Vegans)
<u>SERVES 2-3</u>

Ingredients

1 cup rice
2 cups of water

Method

Measure the rice into a bowl and wash under running water. Drain and keep aside. In a rice cooker bring water to boil [remember to turn the switch to 'cook' mode]. Add the washed rice, stir once and cook covered. When rice is ready the switch changes to 'warm' mode. The rice is ready to be served.

Note: If using a saucepan, bring water to boil, stir in the washed rice and cook covered on low medium heat. Stir often during cooking process to avoid the rice from sticking to the bottom of the pan. If using brown rice use 2 ¼ to 2 ½ cups of water. Brown rice takes longer to cook. Serve the rice with your choice of vegetable or bean curries. Refrigerate the leftovers and reheat well before serving

2. Cumin Rice
(Suitable for Vegans)
<u>SERVES 2 -3</u>

Ingredients

1 cup basmati rice, washed and drained
2 cups water

Seasonings

2 tsp cumin seeds
½" long cinnamon stick
½ tsp salt
Few strands of saffron, if available
2 tsp oil
2 tsp cashews, dry roasted

Method

Place the water with salt and saffron strands in a rice cooker. Bring it to boil. Meanwhile in a stir fry pan, heat the oil and add the cumin seeds and the cinnamon stick. Sauté for a minute and then add the washed rice and sauté on low medium heat for about 2-3 minutes. Now transfer the rice into the rice cooker, stir and let it cook. Garnish with cashew nuts and serve hot.

Note: A saucepan can be used instead of a rice cooker, but the rice needs constant stirring and attention for uniform cooking. This aromatic rice can be served with vegetables or bean curries. Store any unused portion in the refrigerator and reheat well before serving.

Carrot rice

3. Carrot Rice
(Suitable for Vegans)
<u>SERVES 2-3</u>

Ingredients

1 cup basmati rice, washed and drained
2 cups water
4 medium size carrots grated
¼ cup green peas
¼ cup green/red peppers chopped
1 onion thinly sliced

Seasonings

¾ tsp mustard seeds
1 tsp yellow split peas
1"long dried chilli
Less than ¼ tsp turmeric powder
¾ tsp cumin powder
½ tsp ground coriander
¼ tsp pepper powder [optional]
Salt
2 tsp oil
2-3 tsp cilantro leaves finely chopped

Method

Cook the rice and cool it by spreading it on a platter. Keep aside. Heat oil in a skillet and before it smokes add the mustard seeds, yellow split peas, dried red chilli and turmeric powder. When the mustard seeds stop popping, add the onions and fry for about 3 minutes. Now add the grated carrots and sauté it. Cover and cook on low medium heat till the carrots are done. Remove the skillet from heat. Add cooked rice, salt, cumin powder, ground coriander, cooked green peas, chopped raw peppers and cilantro leaves. Mix well using a light hand till the rice is uniform in appearance. If extra spice is needed [as some carrots are very sweet] add the pepper powder. Discard the red chilli before serving.

Note: This rice is easy to make, tasty, healthy and very colorful. Serve it with plain yogurt or yogurt based salads. Refrigerate the leftovers.

4. Cumin Pepper Rice
(Suitable for Vegans)
<u>SERVES 2-3</u>

Ingredients

1 cup basmati rice, washed and drained
2 cups water

Seasonings

2 tsp cumin seeds
½ tsp cumin powder
¼ to ½ tsp pepper powder
½ tsp salt
2 tsp oil
2 tsp of cilantro leaves, finely chopped

Method

Add salt to the water and bring it boil, preferably in a rice cooker. Heat oil in a pan and before it smokes add the cumin seeds, cumin powder and pepper powder. A minute later add the washed rice and roast it for 2-3 minutes. Transfer the rice from the pan to the boiling water, mix well and cook till done. Before serving, spread the rice on a platter and garnish with cilantro leaves. Serve hot.

Note: Traditionally in Indian cooking cumin and pepper go together as the flavors complement each other. Cilantro leaves make this rice more aromatic and colorful. This rice can be served with vegetable, bean curries or yogurt based salads. Please refrigerate the leftovers and reheat well before serving.

5. Masala Rice
(Suitable for Vegans)
SERVES 2-3

Ingredients

1 cup basmati rice, washed and drained
1/3 cup green peas
2 medium sized potatoes cut into cubes
1 medium sized onion finely sliced
2 cups hot water

Seasonings

1 tsp garam masala
Less than ¼ tsp red chilli powder
Less than ¼ tsp turmeric powder
½ tsp ground coriander
½ tsp sugar
3 tsp oil
2 tsp cilantro leaves finely chopped
2 tsp dry coconut powder [if available]
Salt

Method

Fry the potatoes lightly and keep aside. Make a paste with garam masala, red chilli powder, turmeric powder and ground coriander using a little water. Keep aside. Heat oil in a skillet and fry the onions for about 2 minutes, now add the spice paste and fry for a minute. Add the rice and sauté for 2 minutes. Now add hot water, salt, sugar and coconut powder. Mix well and cook covered for about 5 minutes. Now add the fried potatoes and peas and continue to cook till done. Mix lightly to avoid burning and for uniform cooking. Garnish with cilantro leaves before serving. Serve hot.

Note: if you are using rice cooker, bring water to boil along with salt and sugar. Add the sautéed rice to the water, mix well and let it cook. After about 5 minutes, add the fried potatoes and green peas, mix and let it cook till done. Though this rice can be eaten by itself, yogurt or yogurt based salads go well as dip. Store any unused rice in the refrigerator and reheat well before serving.

My aunt Ms. Malati taught me this rice preparation and I really admire and appreciate her culinary skills.

Kashmir pilaf [Rice with dry fruits]

6. Kashmir Pilaf
[Rice with Dry Fruits]
(Suitable for Vegans)
SERVES 2-3

Ingredients

1 cup basmati rice, washed & drained
2 cups water
1 small onion finely sliced
¼ cup green peas

Seasonings

½ tsp cumin seeds
¼ tsp fennel seeds
1"long cinnamon stick
2 cardamom pods
2 cloves
1 bay leaf
1 jalapeno pepper
Few strands saffron
Salt
2 tsp oil

Fresh fruits

4-6 thin slices of red apple [with peel]
4-6 thin slices of firm pears
6-8 cherries [fresh or preserved]

Dry fruits

2 tsp chopped apricot, 2 tsp raisins
2 tsp cashew nut pieces, 2 tsp walnut pieces
2 tsp almond slivered

Preparation before hand

Lightly fry all the dry fruits separately using little oil.
Mix together and keep aside.

Method

Heat oil in a skillet and add cumin, fennel, cinnamon, cardamom, bay leaf, cloves. Sauté for a minute and then add the jalapeno pepper and onions. Fry for about 2 minutes. Now add the rice and sauté for about 2-3 minutes. Add hot water, salt and saffron strands to the skillet, mix well and cook covered on low medium heat. Stir with a light hand often to avoid burning. When rice is about half cooked, add the green peas and cook till done.

Before serving, spread the rice on a platter, pick out the jalapeno pepper, cardamom, cinnamon, cloves and bay leaf and discard it. Mix in the dry fruits, cherries, fresh fruits and serve this rice well decorated.

Note: This rice preparation is from Kashmir, the home of saffron, dry fruits and nuts. This rice tends to be rich and a little heavy to the stomach due to the oily nuts. Smaller serving portion is advised. As this rice is slightly sweet in taste, spicy vegetables can served along with it. The recipe does appear to be complicated due to the lengthy list of ingredients, but it is not so. Please spend a few minutes to organize the seasonings and to prepare the dry fruits, you will be amazed how simple this recipe will seem. Kindly store unused portion in the refrigerator and reheat well before serving.

Lemon rice

7. Lemon Rice
(Suitable for Vegans)
SERVES 2-3

Ingredients

- 1 cup basmati rice, washed and drained
- 2 cups water

Optional

- 4 tsp roasted peanuts
- ¼ cup green peas, cooked
- ¼ cup green and red peppers chopped finely

Seasonings

- ½ tsp mustard seeds
- ¾ tsp cumin seeds
- 1 tsp yellow split peas
- 1"long dried red chilli or 1 small jalapeno pepper slit lengthwise
- ½ tsp grated ginger root or less than ¼ tsp ginger powder
- Less than ¼ tsp turmeric powder
- 2-3 tbsp lemon/ lime juice
- 2 tsp cilantro leaves, finely chopped
- 3 tsp oil
- Salt

Method

Cook rice with ½ tsp salt and a pinch of turmeric powder. Keep aside and cool it. Heat oil in a skillet and before it smokes, add mustard seeds, cumin seeds, yellow split peas, dried chilli, turmeric powder and ginger powder. When the mustard seeds stop popping, remove the skillet from heat and add rice, salt and lemon/lime juice. Mix well in the skillet so that the rice is uniform in taste and color. Sprinkle cilantro leaves before serving. If desired add the peanuts, green peas and peppers for better taste and appearance.

Note: if using jalapeno pepper and fresh ginger, add it to the skillet after the mustard seeds have stopped popping and sauté them for a minute before turning the heat off. This rice is very simple to make though the list of ingredients may appear long. Kindly use your own judgment while adding the lemon/lime juice. This rice will certainly enliven the table due to its color. As always store unused portion in the refrigerator and reheat well before serving.

8. *Mint Potato Rice*
(Suitable for Vegans)
SERVES 2-3

Ingredients

1 cup basmati rice, washed and drained
1 medium size potatoes cubed
¼ cup sweet corn
1 carrot cut into round slices
1 small onion finely sliced
2 cups water

Seasonings

1 tsp cumin seeds
Less than ¼ tsp turmeric powder
1/2 cup chopped mint leaves
1 jalapeno pepper slit lengthwise
3 tsp oil
Salt

Method

Heat oil in a skillet and brown the cumin seeds. Add jalapeno pepper and onions and sauté them till onions are brown. Add the carrots, potatoes, sweet corn, mint leaves and turmeric powder. Sauté for 2 to 3 minutes. Now add the rice and mix well and sauté for 2-3 minutes. Add hot water and salt. Mix well and cook covered till done. Stir occasionally to avoid burning and for uniform taste. Serve hot.

> **Note:** If using rice cooker, bring water to boil along with salt and add the sautéed rice [with spices and vegetable] to the cooker, mix well and let it cook till done. Garnish with a few firm slices of tomato, or slices of lemon or few whole mint leaves. Kindly adjust the amount of mint leaves according to taste. Yogurt based salads go well with this rice, but it can be eaten by itself. Kindly refrigerate any unused portion and reheat well before using.

9. Potato Pepper Rice
(Suitable for Vegans)
SERVES 3

Ingredients

1 cup basmati rice, washed and drained
2 cups water
1 potato cubed
2 peppers [red/green] cut into long pieces
¼ cup lima beans, cooked
1 small onion thinly sliced

Seasonings

¾ tsp mustard seeds
1 tsp yellow split peas
1"long dried red chilli
Less than ¼ tsp turmeric powder
1 tsp curry powder
2 tsp dill leaves finely cut
Salt
3 tsp oil

Method

Cook the rice and cool it by spreading it on a platter. Heat oil in a skillet and before it smokes, add the mustard seeds, yellow split peas, dried chilli and turmeric powder. When the mustard seeds stop popping, add the onions and sauté for about 2 minutes. Now add the potatoes and pepper, let it cook uncovered. When potatoes are more than half way done, add the curry powder and dill leaves and let it cook till potatoes are crisp and cooked. Remove the skillet from heat and add rice, salt and lima beans, mix well using a light hand. Discard the chilli before serving.

Note: Serve preferably with yogurt based salads. Refrigerate the leftovers and reheat well before serving.

10. Rice with Split Peas
(Suitable for Vegans)
<u>SERVES 2-3</u>

Ingredients

¾ cup rice, rinsed and drained

1/3 cup green and yellow split peas [combined]

2 ¼ cup of hot water

Seasonings

¾ tsp mustard seeds

1 tsp cumin seeds

¼ tsp turmeric powder

¼-1/2 tsp pepper powder

¼-1/2 tsp cumin powder

1 tsp fresh grated ginger or less than ¼ tsp ginger powder

Salt

2 tsp oil

2 tsp cilantro leaves, finely chopped

Method

Rinse the split peas and cook it with little water in a microwave oven [for 3 minutes] or on stove top [for about 5 minutes]. Keep aside. Heat oil in a skillet or a pan and before it smokes add the mustard seeds and the cumin seeds. When the mustard seeds stop popping, add turmeric powder and the ginger. Now add the rinsed rice, slightly cooked split peas, pepper powder and the cumin powder. Sauté for about 3 to 4 minutes on low medium heat. Now you can choose any of the following methods to proceed.

1. Add hot water and salt stir well and let it cook till rice and peas are cooked to a soft consistency. Stir few times during cooking to avoid burning and add little water if required.

2. Place water for boiling in a rice cooker and transfer all the ingredients from the pan/skillet. Add salt, stir well and cook till rice and peas are cooked well.

3. If using a pressure cooker, you can eliminate the precooking of the split peas. Season and sauté all the ingredients in the pressure cooker, add water and salt, stir well and cook till done.

Sprinkle cilantro leaves before serving. Serve the hot rice with chilled yogurt or yogurt based salads.

> **Note:** Personally I prefer the pressure cooker method as the rice and peas are well cooked and it eliminates using an additional pan/skillet and also I can avoid precooking the peas. In India rice and split mung beans are cooked with spices and it is called 'khichidi'. This rice is prepared all over India with slight variation from region to region. This rice is considered a simple fare and popular as it becomes one dish meal. Please refrigerate any leftovers and reheat well before serving.

11. *Seasoned Rice*
(Suitable for Vegans)
<u>SERVES 2-3</u>

Ingredients

1 cup rice, washed and drained
2 cups water
1 small onion finely chopped

Seasonings

1 tsp mustard seeds
1 tsp cumin seeds
1 tsp yellow split peas
1"long dried red chilli or small jalapeno pepper slit lengthwise
2 tsp cilantro leaves
3 tsp oil
Salt

Method

Add 1/2 tsp of salt to the water and cook the rice in saucepan or rice cooker. Keep aside and let it cool [preferably spread it on a platter]. Heat oil in a stir fry pan and before it smokes add the mustard seeds, cumin seeds, yellow split peas and dried chilli. When the mustard seeds stop popping add the onions and sauté till brown. Remove the skillet from heat and add rice and little salt and mix well using a light hand. Garnish with cilantro leaves before serving.

Tomato pepper rice

12. Tomato Pepper Rice
(Suitable for Vegans)
<u>SERVES 2-3</u>

Ingredients

1 cup basmati rice, washed and drained
2 cups water
3 medium size tomatoes, diced
2 green peppers cut into long pieces
1 small onion finely sliced

Seasonings

¾ tsp mustard seeds
1 tsp yellow split peas
2 cloves
2 cardamom pods
1"long cinnamon stick
2" long dried red chilli
¼ tsp turmeric powder
Salt
2-3 tsp oil
2 tsp cilantro leaves finely cut

Method

Cook the rice along with cloves, cinnamon stick and cardamom pods. Keep aside, cool and pick out the spices and discard it. Heat oil in a skillet and before it smokes add the mustard seeds, yellow split peas and the dried chilli. When the seeds stop spluttering, add the onions and turmeric powder and let the onions brown. Now add the peppers and tomatoes and let it cook uncovered till tomatoes soften. Peppers can remain slightly crisp and crunchy. Remove from heat and add the rice and salt and mix well. Garnish with cilantro leaves before serving.

Note: Serve with yogurt or yogurt based salads. Refrigerate the leftovers.

Vegetable pilaf

13. Vegetable Pilaf
(Suitable for Vegans)
<u>SERVES 3</u>

Ingredients

1 cup basmati rice, washed and drained
2 cups of mixed vegetables [carrots, peppers, peas, corn, green beans, potato, cauliflower]
1 onion thinly sliced
2 cups of hot water

Seasonings

1 tsp cumin seeds
½ tsp fennel seeds
2 cardamom pods
2 cloves
1"long cinnamon stick
1 bay leaf
1 jalapeno pepper slit lengthwise
3 tsp oil
Few mint leaves
Less than ¼ tsp ginger powder or 1 tsp grated ginger
Less than ¼ tsp garlic powder or 1 garlic clove chopped
A dash of turmeric powder
Salt

Method

Heat oil in a skillet and before it smokes add cumin seeds, fennel seeds, cloves, cinnamon, cardamom, bay leaf and jalapeno pepper. After a minute, add the ginger, garlic and onions. Sauté for about 2 minutes. Now add all the vegetables and mint leaves and cook for a couple of minutes. Add the rice and sauté till rice becomes slightly transparent. Now add hot water and salt mix well and cook covered on low medium heat, turning it often to avoid burning. Remove from heat when rice is done. Spread it on a platter; pick out the spices like jalapeno pepper, cinnamon, cloves, cardamom and bay leaf. If desired garnish with roasted cashew nuts and serve hot.

Note: If using a rice cooker, bring water to boil with salt and add all the ingredients from the skillet. Mix well and let it cook. This is easier as you don't need to keep an eye on it. Serve with yogurt based salads, vegetable curries or bean curries. Organizing all the required spices beforehand in a small cup is recommended. Store unused portion in the refrigerator.

14. Whole Spice Rice
(Suitable for Vegans)
<u>SERVES 3</u>

Ingredients

1 cup basmati rice, washed and drained
2 cups water
¼ cup green peas
½ cup peppers finely chopped [green, red and yellow]

Seasonings

2 whole cloves
2 cardamom pods
1"long cinnamon stick
1 bay leaf
4-6 black peppercorns
1 tsp cumin seeds
½ tsp fennel seeds
2 tsp oil
Salt

Method

Add ½ tsp of salt to the water and bring it to boil in a saucepan or rice cooker. Meanwhile heat oil in a skillet and before it smokes add all the spices and sauté for a minute or two. Now add the rice and sauté for another 2-3 minutes. Add the rice along with the spices to the boiling water. Stir well and let it cook covered till done. Microwave the peas with little water for a minute and keep aside. Spread the cooked rice in a platter or a shallow dish, pick out cloves, cardamom, cinnamon, bay leaf and peppercorns and discard it. Drain the peas and add it to the rice along with the chopped peppers. Mix lightly and serve.

> **Note:** this aromatic rice can be served with vegetables, beans, yogurt based salad or just plain yogurt. Please store leftovers in the refrigerator and reheat well before serving.

15. Yogurt Rice
(Not Suitable for Vegans)
SERVES 3

Ingredients

1 cup rice [avoid basmati rice as it is non starchy]
2 1/2 cups water
2 cups PLAIN yogurt
1 cup milk [approximately]

Seasonings

1 tsp mustard seeds
½ tsp cumin seeds
1 tsp yellow split peas
¼ tsp ginger powder or ½ tsp fresh grated ginger
1" long jalapeno pepper slit lengthwise
2 tsp oil
Salt
2 tsp cilantro leaves finely chopped

Method

Cook the rice with a pinch of salt. Cool it in a bowl. In a small pan heat the oil and before it smokes add the mustard seeds, cumin seeds and yellow split peas. When the mustard seeds stop spluttering, add the jalapeno pepper and ginger. Remove from heat and pour this seasoning over the rice. When the seasoning cools, add salt and mash the rice coarsely using a big spoon or masher. Whisk the plain yogurt and add it to the rice and mix well. You might need to add little water or milk to bring it to a semi solid consistency. Pick out the jalapeno pepper, discard it and cool the rice preferably by adding a few ice cubes to it. Serve garnished with cilantro leaves.

Note: Depending on the variety of rice, there is a possibility of the rice hardening. Just add little water, milk or yogurt and mix well till desired consistency is achieved. If desired toss in ½ cup of finely chopped cucumbers or 4 tsp of pomegranate seeds just before serving. Enjoy this strange dish on a hot day.

Important-use only plain yogurt.

Webster's New World College Dictionary defines salad as 'a dish usually cold, of raw or sometimes cooked vegetables or fruits in various combinations, served with a dressing'. Traditionally Indian meals included salad, but somewhere along the way salads made their presence only on special occasions. The reason was either economic and or the women were overworked with household chores and hence omitted salads from the meal as it involved lot of chopping, cutting, grating and so on. But of late people have realized the nutritional value of salads and salads do help in reducing a person's weight and even to keep it off. Excess body weight leads to health issues and hence salads play a vital role in healthy life style.

Before globalization vegetables like lettuce, celery, and broccoli were not available everywhere in India. When I was growing up we had salads prepared with cucumbers, carrots, tomatoes, onions, radish, sprouts and lentils. Generally the dressing comprised of oil based seasonings, Yogurt, cilantro leaves, mint leaves, grated coconut, slices of raw mango and lime juice.

I had seen pictures of lettuce, celery, broccoli in foreign cookbooks, but saw them for the first time in 1993 in Zurich. I was completely clueless as to how to eat it and language being a barrier I did not attempt to explore this part of the produce world. It was in this country that I was adventurous enough to try some of these 'exotic' vegetables. Now I am able to mix and match these vegetables with a hint of spices. Salads play the role of natural coolant for the digestive system; hence I prefer to keep the spice level low.

Yogurt based salads are known as 'raita'. These are excellent side dishes to all the spicy rice preparations and bean curries. Generally Indians are not vegans and hence yogurt and yogurt based salads are almost mandatory in our meals. This is again due to the fact that yogurt aids digestion. Further religious and climatic conditions play a role in making yogurt an important part of the meal. Indian population being predominantly Hindu, consider cow 'Holy' and hence the reverence to all dairy products.

Further the heat, dust and humidity makes yogurt and buttermilk an important aspect of our culinary style. Yet we have some rules were yogurt can be used and not. This is based on scientific reasons as to why certain foods should not be in the vicinity of milk or yogurt. Even today some conservative families follow these rules, but I don't follow it strictly as it sometimes cumbersome, though it is scientifically correct.

This section was the most difficult to write, though salads are considered as easy to make. The possibilities are endless and I had to combine the eastern and western culinary ideas. But I did enjoy the number of hours I spent in thinking and translating it into action. I was fortunate to meet Mr. Steve Meyerowitz 'the sproutman' at a meeting of the Northern Connecticut Vegetarian Society. He opened a new amazing world of sprouts. I was accustomed to eating only 'moong bean' sprouts, but the chance encounter enhanced my knowledge and curiosity about sprouts.

In the following pages I have written few recipes using vegetables, lentils, sprouts and beans. They are simple to make, yet delicious and nutritious. I have devoted a small section to yogurt based salads which are NOT suitable for vegans. Enjoy the salads with a meal or as a snack. If you like yogurt, you will certainly enjoy the yogurt based salads and appreciate the benefits of it especially on a hot day.

1. *Carrot Salad*
(Suitable for Vegans)
<u>SERVES 2</u>

Ingredients

    2 cups grated carrots
    4 tbsp yellow split peas, soaked in warm water for an hour and drained

Seasonings

    ½ tsp mustard seeds
    1/2" long dried red chilli or 1"long jalapeno pepper
    Salt
    1 tsp oil
    A generous dash of lemon/lime juice
    1 tsp finely cut cilantro leaves

Method

Place the drained yellow split peas and grated carrots in a bowl. Heat oil in a small pan and before it smokes add the mustard seeds and dried chilli. Cover and when mustard seeds stop popping, pour this seasoning over the carrots. Mix well, cover and chill for an hour. Just before serving add the salt, lime juice and cilantro leaves and toss well. Discard the chilli.

Note: If using jalapeno pepper, add it to the oil after the mustard seeds have stopped popping and let it cook in the oil for less than a minute. To maintain crispness of the salad add salt and lime juice just before serving. Always refrigerate the leftovers and enjoy it later as a snack or with a meal.

2. Carrot-Cucumber with Sprouts
(Suitable for Vegans)
<u>SERVES 2</u>

Ingredients

1 cucumber peeled and finely chopped
1 carrot grated
1 cup sprouts [any kind]

Seasonings

½ tsp cumin powder
Less than ¼ tsp pepper powder
Salt
A generous dash of lime/lemon juice
2-4 mint leaves finely chopped

Method

In a bowl combine chopped cucumbers, grated carrot, sprouts, cumin powder, pepper powder and mint leaves. Mix well, cover and chill. Before serving add salt and lime juice and toss well.

Note: You will notice the absence of oil in this preparation. I deliberately omit it occasionally. Enjoy this nutritious salad as a snack or with a meal. Kindly refrigerate the leftovers.

3. Cucumber Salad
(Suitable for Vegans)
<u>SERVES 2</u>

Ingredients

1 cucumber peeled and finely cut
4 tbsp yellow split peas, soaked in warm water for an hour and then drained

Seasonings

1 tsp mustard seeds
¼ tsp cumin powder
1"long dried red chilli
1 tsp oil
Salt
A generous dash of lemon/ lime juice
2 tsp cilantro leaves finely chopped

Method

Place the chopped cucumber and split peas in a bowl. Sprinkle cumin powder and mix well. Heat oil in a small pan and before it smokes add the mustard seeds and dried red chilli. Cover and when the mustard seeds stop popping, pour the seasoning over the cucumbers. Mix well, cover and chill. Just before serving add salt, lemon/lime juice and cilantro leaves and mix well. Discard the chilli before serving.

Note: The addition of cumin powder helps relieve the discomfort some experience on eating cucumbers. Enjoy this salad as a snack or as a part of the meal. Please refrigerate the leftovers.

Mixed bean vegetable Salad

4. Mixed Bean Vegetable Salad

(Suitable for Vegans)

SERVES 2-3

Ingredients

¼ cup cooked kidney beans
¼ cup cooked chick peas
1 tomato diced
1 small cucumber chopped into slices
1 carrot grated
Few leaves of lettuce, shredded
¼ cup fresh pomegranate seeds
[if available]

Seasonings

1/2tsp mustard seeds
1 tsp yellow split peas
A pinch of ginger powder
1"long dried red chilli
2 tsp oil
Salt
2-3 tsp cilantro leaves finely chopped

Method

Soak kidney beans and chick peas separately for about 8 hours. Drain and wash it well and pressure cook it separately. If not use canned kidney beans and chick peas as it is more convenient. Heat oil in a pan and before it smokes add the mustard seeds, yellow split peas, dried chilli and ginger powder. Once the mustard seeds stop spluttering add the kidney beans and chick peas and a little salt. Reduce the heat and cook for a few minutes. Sprinkle little water if required. Transfer these into a small bowl, cover and keep aside. Combine the cucumber slices, grated carrots and lettuce in a salad bowl and chill. Before you serve add freshly diced tomatoes, cooked beans, little salt and cilantro leaves. Mix well with a light hand. Sprinkle the pomegranate seeds if available. Serve immediately.

Note: This salad is more filling due to the beans. Always add fresh cut tomatoes just before serving. This will help the crispness of the salad. If desired you can add a few broccoli florets too.

Pomegranate seeds-pomegranate is now considered exotic and we find pomegranate juice and herbal pomegranate tea etc in the super market. Dried pomegranate seeds have been used as a spice in Indian cuisine from ages. We had a pomegranate tree while I was growing up and I have enjoyed the fruit immensely. Even now whenever available I buy it, cut it into 4 quarters and remove the seeds using fingers and store it in an air tight box in the refrigerator and my children take it to school as a snack. I admit the process is little messy but worth the trouble. These deep red seeds can make an ordinary salad into an 'exotic' one.

Sprinkle little salt and a dash of pepper powder on pomegranate seeds and enjoy this tasty snack.

Mixed Vegetable Salad

5.Mixed Vegetable Salad
(Suitable for Vegans)
SERVES 2-3

Ingredients

3 cups of chopped vegetables [cucumbers, carrots, celery, lettuce, radish, peppers]

1 tomato diced

¾ cup broccoli florets [microwave for a minute]

½ cup tofu cubes

Seasonings

1 tsp mustard seeds

½ tsp cumin powder

2 tsp yellow split peas

2"long dried red chilli

Salt

2 tsp oil

2-3 tsp lime juice

3 tsp cilantro leaves finely chopped

Method

Combine all vegetables [except tomatoes], tofu cubes and cumin powder in a bowl. Cover and chill. Before serving, heat oil in a small pan and before it smokes add mustard seeds, yellow split peas and dried chilli. Cover. When mustard seeds stop spluttering pour this seasoning over the vegetables. Add tomatoes salt, lime juice and cilantro leaves and mix well with a light hand. Discard the chilli and serve.

Note: if desired microwave ½ to 1 cup of broccoli florets and toss it in the salad. The green color brightens up the salad and makes it appear very appetizing. As always refrigerate the left overs.

Yogurt based salads are NOT suitable for vegans. Yogurt has been an important part of Indian cuisine from time immemorial. Yogurt has proved to be beneficial in the process of digestion and general health of the digestive system. The food we eat is spicy and oily and yogurt makes this kind of food easy on the stomach. Further yogurt has a tremendous cooling effect on the body especially in hot weather.

In India yogurt is made at home on a daily basis. Even in this country I make yogurt almost every day. The taste of fresh homemade yogurt is very good. The key to making good firm yogurt is the culture. To make yogurt bring a pint of milk to boil. 2% milk is good enough. [Whole milk is too rich, while 1% and skim is too watery]. Cool the milk till it is tepid or luke warm. Add 2 tbsp of yogurt culture stir the milk well and set in a warm place. Steel bowl is preferable to set the yogurt, if not use a pre warmed/preheated glass bowl. It will set in 5-7 hours. Once set, refrigerate it.

The problem you might face is getting the starter culture. If you have any Indian family in the neighborhood, feel free to ask them for the starter culture. Though you may not know them, it is perfectly fine to ask them and they will be very happy to give it to you.

The other alternative is to use yogurt which has active/live culture. Once you set the yogurt, keep aside 2 tbsp of it for the next time you set. In case you lose the culture, don't hesitate to ask for it again. You can get it from any Indian restaurant too.

Yogurt based salads are called 'raita'. Generally raita comprises of finely chopped raw vegetables mixed with yogurt and seasoned with mild spices. Yogurt based salads are non spicy preparations as it is intended to cool the digestive system. It is very simple to make and I do hope you too can enjoy the benefits of yogurt in a new preparations. Further many of you might be avoiding the fruit based yogurts as they are high in sugars, this may be an alternative for you.

A word of advice- please use only PLAIN yogurt in the following recipes and not flavored ones. Salt is generally added to the raw vegetables raitas just before serving to prevent the vegetables from turning soggy. A few tsp of sour cream can be added to make these raitas taste rich and delicious. A little water too can be added if the yogurt salad is too thick.

1. Cucumber in Yogurt
(Not Suitable for Vegans)
SERVES 2

Ingredients

1 cup grated or finely chopped cucumbers

1 ½ cups well beaten yogurt

Seasonings

¾ tsp mustard seeds

1 tsp yellow split peas

1 small jalapeno pepper, slit lengthwise or

1" long dried red chilli

1 tsp oil

Salt

1 tsp finely chopped cilantro leaves

Method

In a bowl place the grated/chopped cucumbers. Heat oil in a small pan and before it smokes add the mustard seeds and the yellow split peas. Cover. When the mustard seeds stop spluttering, add the jalapeno pepper and remove from heat. Pour this over the cucumbers, mix well, cover and chill. Just before serving add salt and the well beaten yogurt, cilantro leaves and mix well. Discard the chilli and enjoy.

Note: if using dry red chilli, add it to the oil along with the mustard seeds and split peas. Adjust the quantity of yogurt depending on the consistency and preference. Little water too can be added. This is an excellent accompaniment to all spicy rice dishes and bean curries. This can be enjoyed as a snack on a hot, humid day instead of sugar rich fruit yogurt. Store any leftover portion in the refrigerator.

2.Potato & Spices in Yogurt
(Not Suitable for Vegans)
<u>SERVES 2-3</u>

Ingredients

2 medium sized potatoes, boiled, peeled
and cut into small pieces
1 ½ to 2 cups well beaten yogurt

Seasonings

1 tsp mustard seeds
½ tsp cumin seeds
½ tsp cumin powder
1"long dried chilli
2 tsp oil
Salt
2 tsp finely chopped cilantro leaves
Or
2-3 mint leaves finely chopped

Method

Place the boiled, peeled and chopped potatoes in a bowl. Sprinkle cumin powder and salt. Mix well. Heat oil in a small pan and before it smokes add the mustard seeds, cumin seeds, and red chilli. Cover. When the mustard seeds stop spluttering, pour the seasoning over the potatoes, mix well, cover and chill. Before serving add the yogurt, cilantro/mint leaves and mix well. Discard the chilli.

Note: Salt and spices are added in the initial process so that the flavors can get infused into the potatoes. You may add a little water if required. Store any unused portion in the refrigerator. This recipe is similar to the potato salads available in Deli, except slightly spicier.

Cucumber, tomato & onion in yogurt

3. Cucumber, Tomato & Onion in Yogurt
(Not Suitable for Vegans)
SERVES 2-3

Ingredients

1 small cucumber finely chopped
1 tomato diced
1 small onion finely chopped
1 ½ cups well beaten yogurt

Seasonings

1 tsp mustard seeds
½ tsp cumin powder
1" long dried red chilli
2 tsp finely chopped cilantro leaves
Salt
2 tsp oil

Method

Place cucumbers, tomatoes and onion in a bowl and sprinkle cumin powder. Heat oil in a small pan and before it smokes add the mustard seeds and the dried red chilli. Cover. When the mustard seeds stop popping, remove from heat and pour it over the vegetables. Mix well. Cover and chill. Before you serve add salt, yogurt, cilantro leaves and mix well. Discard the red chilli and enjoy.

Note: You can omit the raw onions or substitute it with finely chopped red and green peppers. Refrigerate any unused portions.

Cucumber-cumin in yogurt

4. Cucumber-Cumin in Yogurt

(Not Suitable for Vegans)

<u>SERVES 2-3</u>

Ingredients

1 cup finely chopped cucumbers
1 ½ cups well beaten yogurt

Seasonings

½ tsp cumin powder
Less than ¼ tsp ground pepper
Salt
3 to 4 fresh mint leaves, finely chopped or a generous dash of dry mint leaves

Method

Place the chopped cucumbers in a bowl and sprinkle cumin powder and the pepper powder. Mix well and chill. Before serving add yogurt, salt and mint leaves.

Note: Serve this preparation with spicy rice and bean curries. The combination of cumin, pepper, yogurt and mint leaves helps in relieving any stomach discomfort experienced after heavy or spicy meal. Store unused portion in the refrigerator.

5. Spinach & Sweet Corn in Yogurt
(Not Suitable for Vegans)
SERVES 2-3

Ingredients

1 cup cooked spinach
½ cup cooked sweet corn
1 to 1 1/2 cup well beaten yogurt

Seasonings

1 tsp mustard seeds
1 tsp yellow split peas
Less than ¼ tsp ginger powder
¼ tsp cumin powder
1" long dried red chilli
2 tsp oil
Salt

Method

In a bowl place cooked spinach and sweet corn and sprinkle cumin powder. Heat oil in a small pan and before it smokes add the mustard seeds, yellow split peas and dried red chilli. Cover. When the mustard seeds stop spluttering, add the ginger powder to the oil and remove from heat. Pour this seasoning over the spinach-sweet corn, add salt and mix well. Cover and chill. Before serving add the yogurt and mix well. Discard the chilli and enjoy.

Note: serve this salad with any rice preparation or enjoy as a snack any time. Refrigerate the leftovers.

Introduction

Beans and peas are seeds in a pod from leguminous plants. This section of the book deals with dried beans and peas. Beans are very rich in protein and are often substituted for meat. This nutritional fact makes beans an important part of vegetarian diet.

Beans are used in different cuisines all over the world. They are used in soups, salads, curries, cooked with rice and so on. Being vegetarian by birth I ate lots of varieties of beans cooked in different ways. Unfortunately I am not able to share all those delicious and nutritious recipes as I have no idea what those beans are called in the English language nor are they available in a regular American supermarket.

This led me to explore another world of beans and I was able to create recipes with the beans available in the local supermarket. I did put in a lot of thought, experimented with them, coaxed my family into trying them and finally I can say confidently that the outcome was more than satisfactory.

Cooking beans may prove to be cumbersome to many, and may resort to canned beans. I am sure they are very convenient and good. Frankly I have never used canned beans and peas. As I have lots of time on my hands and a tendency to plan ahead, I soak the beans overnight, rinse well and pressure cook it. This method has worked well for me and each one adopts the most convenient method. There is no wrong or right about it. Simplifying cooking should be one of the factors guiding us in our busy life. Though beans have lots of positive aspects about it, we have to acknowledge its major negative aspect. Eating beans gives rise to gas and this fact alone discourages many of us from eating it.

As I have mentioned before that Indian cooking is based on the science of ayurveda, the old wise people of the bygone era discovered that using spices helped in reducing the gas that beans produce. Spices are used not just to enhance the taste but also for the medical benefits they possess. The spices that are commonly used are asafoetida, cumin, ginger and garlic. The usage of these spices helps in easy digestion of the beans.

Slow cooking [crock pot] makes bean dishes tastier as the spices get infused into the beans and there is uniformity in taste and consistency. I use crock pot and pressure cooker for cooking beans. If I have lot of time and the quantity is large, I prefer the crock pot. Sometimes I pressure cook the beans and transfer it to the crock pot and add the spices and other ingredients and let it cook slowly. With crock pot constant attention is not required and the bean curries remain warm till it is ready to be served.

Using your own judgment please decide as to what kind of cookware is most convenient and best suited to you. Though there is a difference in taste depending on the type of cooking, I feel one should not get bogged down by this. Convenience and simplicity should be the watch word in our daily life, while we can use elaborate techniques of cooking for special occasions.

In the following pages I have written down some recipes, some of which have been modified from the traditional, while some are my own creations. You don't have to follow my ideas completely, feel free to omit, add or substitute any ingredient depending on preference or allergies. I sincerely hope you can enjoy beans in different ways and take advantage of the nutrients.

1. Black-eyed Peas
(Suitable for Vegans)
SERVES 2-3

Ingredients

1 ½-2 cups cooked black-eyed peas
1 small onion finely sliced
1 tomato diced

Seasonings

1 tsp cumin seeds
1 tsp curry powder
¼ tsp red chilli powder
½ tsp grated ginger or less than ¼ tsp
   ginger powder
Less than ¼ tsp turmeric powder
Salt
2 tsp oil
2 tsp cilantro leaves finely chopped

Method

Cook the black-eyed peas either in a saucepan, pressure cooker or use canned ones. Keep aside. Heat oil in a skillet and add the cumin seeds. When the cumin seeds brown, add the onions and ginger and sauté for 3-4 minutes. Now add the tomatoes, curry powder, chilli powder, turmeric powder and cook covered with little water. When tomatoes soften add the cooked black-eyed peas, salt, little water and mash lightly with a potato masher. Cook covered on low medium heat till the curry is has a uniform consistency and taste. Add water as required. Garnish with cilantro leaves before serving.

> **Note:** This curry is very easy to prepare and tastes delightful with plain rice, flat bread or warm hamburger buns. Refrigerate or freeze any leftovers and reheat well before serving.

2. Chick Peas - Simple
(Suitable for Vegans)
<u>SERVES 2-3</u>

Ingredients

2 cups of cooked chick peas
1 medium size onion finely chopped
1 large tomato diced

Seasonings

¾ tsp mustard seeds
1 tsp cumin seeds
1 tsp curry powder
¼ tsp red chilli powder
Less than ¼ tsp turmeric powder
Salt
2 tsp oil
2 tsp finely chopped cilantro leaves

Method

Cook the chick peas in the method you feel most convenient or used canned peas. Keep aside. Heat oil in a skillet and before it smokes add the mustard seeds and the cumin seeds. When the mustard seeds stop popping, add the onions and sauté till brown. Now add the tomatoes, curry powder, turmeric powder, red chilli powder and cook covered on low medium heat for few minutes. Add little water if the tomatoes dry out. When tomatoes are soft, add the cooked chick peas, salt and little water. Mash the chick peas lightly with a potato masher. Mix well and continue to cook covered on low medium heat for about 8 to 10 minutes. Garnish with cilantro leaves and serve hot.

> Note: These chick peas can be served with any kind of rice and flat breads. Please refrigerate or freeze the leftovers and reheat well, preferably on stove top before serving.

3. Chick Peas - Dry
(Suitable for Vegans)
<u>SERVES 2-3</u>

Ingredients

2 cups of cooked chick peas

Seasonings

¾ tsp mustard seeds
1 tsp yellow split peas
Less than ¼ tsp turmeric powder
1"long dried red chilli
A dash of ginger powder or ½ tsp of
  grated ginger
Salt
2 tsp oil
2 tsp finely chopped cilantro leaves
A dash of lime juice

Method

Cook the chick peas in the method convenient to you or use canned peas. Keep aside. Heat oil in a skillet and before it smokes add the mustard seeds, yellow split peas and the dried red chilli. When the mustard seeds stop sputtering, add ginger, turmeric powder, cooked chick peas and salt. Reduce the heat, stir well and cook covered for about 5 minutes. Before serving add the lime juice and the cilantro leaves. Discard the chilli.

4. Chick Peas in Gravy
(Suitable for Vegans)
<u>SERVES 4</u>

Ingredients

2 cups cooked chick peas

1 medium size onion finely sliced

2-3 large tomatoes diced

Seasonings

1 tsp cumin seeds
½ tsp fennel seeds
2 bay leaves
1 flake garlic chopped or less than ¼ tsp garlic
   powder
¼ tsp red chilli powder
Less than ¼ tsp turmeric powder
1 tsp garam masala
A dash of cinnamon powder
A dash of clove powder
A dash of nutmeg powder
3-4 tsp oil
3 tsp finely chopped cilantro leaves
Salt
Couple of thin lime wedges [optional]

Method

Cook the chick peas in the manner you are most comfortable or used canned ones. Keep aside. Heat oil in a skillet and before it smokes add the cumin seeds, fennel seeds and the bay leaf. When the seeds brown add the onion, ginger and garlic and sauté till the onions brown lightly. Now add the tomatoes, turmeric powder, chilli powder, garam masala, nutmeg powder, cinnamon powder and clove powder. Add little water, mix well and let it cook covered till tomatoes soften. Now add the cooked chick peas, salt and little more water if needed. Lightly mash the chick peas with a potato masher and let it cook covered on low medium heat for about 10 to 15 minutes. Stir often for uniform cooking and taste. Garnish with cilantro leaves and lime wedges and serve hot.

> **Note:** If you want make it for more than 8 servings, it is advisable to use a crock pot. After you add the chick peas and salt to the skillet transfer the entire contents to crock pot, add little water, mix well and let it cook for 3 to 4 hours. These chick peas' taste really good as the spices get infused into the peas. Serve with any kind of rice or flat breads. Store any unused portion in the refrigerator or freezer and reheat well preferably on a stovetop before serving.

5. Edamame [Soy Beans]
(Suitable for Vegans)
<u>SERVES 2-3</u>

Ingredients

1 cup shelled Edamame

Seasonings

½ tsp mustard seeds
1 tsp yellow split peas
A dash or two red chilli powder
Salt
1 tsp oil
1 tsp cilantro leaves finely chopped

Method

Place edamame in salt water in a small saucepan and bring it to boil. When the beans are soft and tender, drain and keep aside. Heat oil in a pan and before it smokes add the mustard seeds and yellow split peas. When the mustard seeds stop spluttering, add the edamame, red chilli powder and salt, if needed. Mix well with a light hand and let it cook for about 2-3 minutes. Sprinkle cilantro leaves before serving.

Note: Please store any unused portion in the refrigerator and heat well before serving.

7. Lentil Soup (With Spices & Vegetables)

(Suitable for Vegans)

SERVES 3-4

Ingredients

½ cup lentils

¼ cup carrots diced

Less than ¼ cup scallions chopped

½ cup tomatoes diced

8-10 oz V8 vegetable juice or Bolthouse farms carrot juice

Seasonings

A dash of garlic powder

A dash of salt

A dash black pepper powder

Method

Cook the lentils till soft, use either a pressure cooker or a saucepan. Keep aside. Combine carrots, scallions and tomatoes in a saucepan with just enough water and cook till tomatoes soften. Add the cooked lentils, dash of garlic powder and lightly mash it with a masher. Add the V8 vegetable juice or Bolthouse farm carrot juice, reduce heat and let it simmer for about 5 minutes. Taste a spoonful before adding salt and pepper powder. Enjoy a bowl of hot soup for lunch or even as a snack.

> **Note:** If using spicy V8 vegetable juice you can eliminate the salt and the pepper completely. Mashing the lentils makes the consistency of the soup uniform. As always refrigerate any unused portion and reheat well before serving.

Kidney beans

6. Kidney Beans
(Suitable for Vegans)
SERVES 2-3

Ingredients

2 cups of cooked kidney beans
1 medium sized onion finely chopped
1 large tomato diced

Seasonings

1 tsp cumin seeds
1 flake garlic chopped or less than ¼ tsp garlic powder
1 tsp grated ginger or less than ¼ tsp ginger powder
1 tsp garam masala
Less than ¼ tsp turmeric powder
¼ tsp red chilli powder
Salt
2 tsp oil
2 tsp finely chopped cilantro leaves

Method

Cook the red kidney beans to a soft consistency or used canned ones. Heat oil in a skillet or a pressure cooker and before it smokes add the cumin seeds. When the cumin seeds brown, add the ginger, garlic and onions. Sauté the onions till done and add the tomatoes, garam masala, turmeric powder and the red chilli powder. Cook till tomatoes soften, add little water if required. Now add the kidney beans, salt and water and mix well and cook covered till the entire curry is well blended. If using a pressure cooker, let some pressure build. When done garnish with cilantro leaves and serve hot.

Note: I have always soaked the kidney beans for 8 to 10 hours and then pressure cooked the beans. This method ensures that the beans cook really well and it is more economical for me to buy the beans and cook instead of canned ones. I keep the cooked beans aside in a bowl and use the same cooker to sauté all other ingredients. Then I add the beans and pressure cook for a few minutes to ensure it is well cooked.

As I spend quite a bit of time and effort, I prefer to make more and freeze a considerable portion for future use. This not only saves time but also energy [helps cut electricity bill]. Further this bean curry freezes well without noticeable change in taste and consistency. Reheat well, preferably on stovetop before serving. Serve with flat bread or rice.

Yellow split peas

9. *Yellow & Green Split Peas*
(Suitable for Vegans)
SERVES 2-3

Ingredients

½ cup uncooked yellow split peas
¼ cup uncooked green split peas

Seasonings

½ tsp mustard seeds
½ tsp cumin seeds
Less than ¼ tsp red chilli powder
Less than ¼ tsp turmeric powder
¾ tsp coriander powder
¼ tsp cumin powder
Salt
2 tsp oil
2 tsp finely chopped cilantro leaves

Method

Cook the yellow split peas till soft and tender. Mash it and keep it aside. Cook the green split peas till tender, DO NOT MASH IT. Keep aside. In a small bowl combine turmeric powder, chilli powder, coriander powder, cumin powder with a little water to make a paste. Keep aside. Heat oil in a saucepan or a skillet and before it smokes add the mustard seeds and the cumin seeds. When the mustard seeds stop spluttering, reduce the heat and carefully add the spice paste. Sauté for a minute, add little water if needed. Now carefully add the mashed yellow split peas, salt and mix well. Let it cook covered for 3 to 4 minutes. Now add the green split peas. Mix well and let it cook covered for another 2 to 3 minutes. Stir often to avoid burning. Garnish with cilantro leaves before serving.

> **Note:** Though I am very familiar with the yellow split peas, I used the green split peas for the first time. This preparation with peas was very delicious and very easy to make. I used pressure cooker to cook the peas and this simplified my work. We enjoyed this dish by dipping our flat breads into it and also by mixing it with basmati rice. My younger daughter Apoorva aka mini liked it so much that she finished all the leftovers the next day and asked me to make it often as it was very tasty. Her opinion really matters to me as she is not very easy to please and has very firm likes and dislikes. As always please refrigerate or freeze any leftovers and reheat well before serving.

8. Pink Beans
(Suitable for Vegans)
<u>SERVES 2-3</u>

Ingredients

1 ½ cups of cooked pink beans
¼ cup scallions chopped
½ cup chopped green peppers
½ cup diced tomatoes

Seasonings

¾ tsp mustard seeds
1 tsp cumin seeds
1 tsp curry powder
Less than ¼ tsp red chilli powder
Salt
2 tsp oil
2 tsp cilantro leaves finely chopped

Method

Cook the pink beans in the method most suitable to you or used canned ones. Keep aside. Heat oil in a skillet and before it smokes, add the mustard seeds and the cumin seeds. When the mustard seeds stop spluttering, add the scallions, peppers, tomatoes and little water. To this add the curry powder, red chilli powder and cook covered for about 5 to 7 minutes on low medium heat. Now mix in the cooked pink beans and salt, mix well and let it cook covered for another 5 to 7 minutes. Add little water if required. Garnish with cilantro leaves and serve hot.

> **Note:** Honestly I had never eaten pink beans till I made it. I bought it to try it out and so I soaked it, pressured cooked it and then I was clueless. I found some scallions and green peppers in the refrigerator, so I just 'cooked up' a recipe using basic ingredients and the outcome was amazing. When my children asked me next day if there was any leftover pink beans, I knew immediately the experiment was successful.
>
> This gave me confidence to try out new kinds of beans. I have a lot to discover and learn and hopefully I will be able to do so. We enjoyed these beans with flat bread and rice. Please refrigerate or freeze any unused portion and reheat well before serving.

Introduction to Breads

Bread is probably the oldest prepared food in the world, dating back to the Neolithic age. The image that comes to our mind when we think of bread is the process of kneading flour and water into a dough and baking it to perfection. This is the simple and basic concept. But the quest for baking a variety of delicious breads led us to use salt, leavening agents, raising agents, spices herbs etc. Is it a wonder that there are innumerous kinds of breads today?

Bread has been such an important aspect of our life that we use the word in day to day language. We use phrases like 'bread winner of the family', 'earning the daily bread', 'bringing bread to the table', 'breaking the bread together', 'knowing which side of the bread is buttered', 'bread basket' so on and so forth. The word 'bread' does not always necessarily mean bread. It has different meanings depending upon the context. At home my husband is the 'bread winner' and I am the baker, literally.

Bread is a universal food, exceptions might be in some of the East Asian countries. Different countries use different flours from a variety of grains to prepare it. Geography plays an important role in determining the kind of bread native to a region. Whatever is the grain grown in a region, the bread is made from the flour of that grain.

My knowledge of breads was widened while strolling through the streets of European cities, where not only one enjoys the aroma of fresh baked bread but can also feast eyes on a variety of breads baked in a various shapes and displayed most tastefully and artistically.

The breads which I will be writing about are Indian flat breads like roti/chapatti and parathas. I remember my mother kneading dough combining whole wheat flour and water, almost daily. Then she would roll it out and cook on a hot griddle. Sometimes she made flat breads combining two or more kinds of flour, like wheat flour, rice flour, chick pea's flour etc. At times she added herbs and spices to the dough and stuffed potatoes to add variety to the daily fare.

India is a geographical diverse country. The major food crop grown in north India is wheat. Flat breads are the main course in north Indian meals. These breads are usually eaten with vegetables, beans or seasoned lentils. We have to use fingers to eat the flat breads. Many might hesitate to do so, but God did create fingers before man invented the spoon. Tear a piece of flat bread and scoop the vegetables or bean curries with it and eat it. You can use spoon for the vegetables, beans and lentils. If you have been to an Indian restaurant you may be familiar with 'naan' bread. 'Naans' are cooked in a special clay oven called 'tandoor'. As most of us do not have access to it, I will not be including it in the book.

Herb flat breads are aromatic breads. Herbs and greens like fenugreek leaves, cilantro leaves, mint leaves, thyme, dill leaves are added to the flour with a pinch of spices. Sometimes spices are added to the flour to 'spice up' the bread. The most delicious of all the Indian flat breads are the stuffed ones. Potatoes and mixed vegetables are filled into dough and then rolled out and cooked on a flat griddle. These stuffed breads are extremely delicious but labor intensive and time consuming. Hence I do not make it on a regular basis.

Preparing flat breads on a daily basis is cumbersome. I knead enough dough for two meals at a time; refrigerate half of it in an air tight container. Before preparing flat breads with the refrigerated dough, I thaw it on the counter for couple of hours. If I am in a hurry, I place the container in a bowl of hot water. Please take care to see that the water does not enter the closed container. I did try warming the dough in the microwave oven, the result was not satisfactory. It is advisable to avoid the microwave oven.

Experience plays an important part in flat bread making. The dough has to be soft but not too moist. It has to sit at room temperature for a couple of hours before using it. Then the bread has to cook on a hot griddle with or without oil. Initially preparing flat breads might be tiresome, but practice makes it easier.

There will be a bit of a mess on the kitchen counter, but I am sure you will figure out to minimize the mess. I am obsessed with neatness, cleanliness and have no tolerance for clutter and unorganized work space. Hence I am alerting about the possibility of mess during flat bread making as there may be people like me where mess is concerned. I store the dough in the refrigerator to a maximum of 2 days and the prepared breads for nor more than a week. I place the flat breads on a paper towel, roll it up and seal it in a zipper plastic bag and refrigerate it. I heat it on a hot griddle before serving.

Despite some short comings, these whole grain flat breads are 'good' food. Due to high fiber content the bread breaks down slowly in the body and doesn't spike up the blood sugar levels unlike rice. This is especially suited for diabetics. As flat breads are eaten with vegetables, beans, lentil and plain yogurt, the blood sugar levels remain steady instead of ups and downs. In south India rice has always been the staple food grain but rising diabetes and obesity has made many people to switch from rice to wheat.

In the following pages the recipes I have written are easy and practical for today's world. Though the possibilities are endless, I have refrained from doing so as my key watch word is 'simplicity'. As always I have used only the ingredients available in an American supermarket. This is going to be an adventure and little difficult at times, but practice leads to perfection. Enjoy the world of flat breads.

Dough for bread

Steps for making simple flat bread [Roti]

1. Simple Flat Bread [Roti]
(Suitable for Vegans)
SERVING: Makes 8-10

Ingredients

1 cup wheat flour
¾ cup [approximately] warm water
A pinch of salt

2 tsp oil
½ cup wheat flour for rolling

Method

Place 1 cup of wheat flour in a mixing bowl. Add oil and salt and mix it well into the flour using fingers. Add warm water little by little to knead the flour into soft dough. The dough should be soft, elastic and not too moist. Shape the dough into a ball and keep covered for an hour or two. [see picture]

Now divide the dough into 8 to 10 small balls. Keep it covered. Take one ball, roll it into dry flour and place the ball on your palm and press lightly and rotate it with your other palm. Now the ball is slightly flattened. Using a rolling pin, roll the dough out into a circle of approximately 8"in diameter and even thickness. Use dry flour as needed for rolling out. Now you have rolled the roti.

Heat a flat griddle on the large burner of the stove and also heat a flattened cake/cookie cooling metal rack on another large burner. When the griddle is hot, transfer the rolled roti onto to it. Reduce the heat slightly. Move or rotate the roti on the griddle using your finger tips or a piece of folded paper towel. After about 10 seconds you will notice small bubbles forming on the roti. Now flip the roti and rotate the roti on the griddle lightly pressing along the edges. After about 5 to 7 seconds transfer the roti from the griddle to the cooling rack, and the roti will puff up. Using a pair of tongs flip it over and cook it lightly on the other side, for about 5 seconds. Remove the roti from heat and store it in an air tight container lined with paper towel. The paper towel will absorb the steam and keep the rotis soft. Repeat the process for the remaining balls of dough. Enjoy these freshly made rotis with vegetables or bean curries.

Note: The whole process of rolling the roti and cooking it should not take more than 90 seconds. It should take a maximum of 60 seconds to roll and about 30 seconds to cook on the griddle and the rack. Some may feel baffled and disheartened after reading the method of roti making. Make 1 roti at a time and when you feel comfortable you can roll out a few and keep them on wax paper and then cook them one after the other. This way you can save time and fuel.

Please place leftover rotis on a sheet of paper towel and roll it and either store it in an air tight container, zipper plastic bag or wrap it in foil. If you are going to use it within 24 hours, store it at room temperature, if not refrigerate it and reheat on a flat griddle before serving. If you are not vegan, you can lightly brush some clarified butter [ghee] to one side of the hot roti before storing it in the box. [As show in the picture]

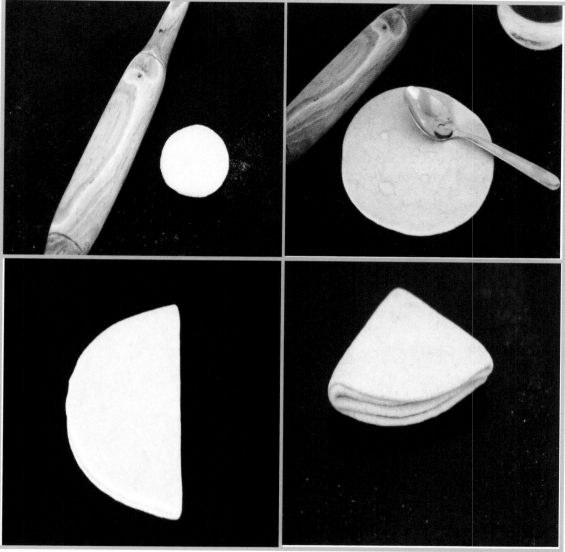

Steps for making layered flat bread

Steps for making layered flat bread (contd.)

2. Layered Flat Bread [Paratha]
(Suitable for Vegans)
<u>SERVING:</u> Makes 6-8

Ingredients

1 cup wheat flour
¾ cup [approximately] warm water
A generous pinch of salt

2 tsp oil for kneading
½ cup wheat flour for rolling
Oil for cooking

Method

Place 1 cup of flour in a mixing bowl and add salt and oil to it. Gently mix the flour well using fingers. Now add warm water little by little to knead the flour into soft, elastic but not too moist dough. Roll the dough into a ball and keep covered for an hour or two.

Divide the dough into 6 to 8 balls of same size and keep covered. Take one ball, roll into dry flour and gently roll it between your palms. Now you have a slightly flattened ball of dough. Place this dough on a board and roll it out to a circle of 4 to 5 inches in diameter. Apply a few drops of oil evenly on the circular dough and fold it into half. Now fold this again into half, you have small triangular dough. Using dry flour as needed roll out this triangular dough to a size of approximately 6 to 7 inches each side. Please try to roll out evenly so that it has uniform thickness. Now this layered bread is ready to be cooked.

Heat a flat griddle and transfer this flat bread to it. Reduce the heat to medium. Gently move the flat bread on the griddle to avoid sticking and burning. In a few seconds you will notice bubbles forming, now flip it and apply few drops of oil to the cooked side. Again flip it back and apply few drops of oil to the other side. Using a spatula or a turner gently press along the edges to cook well. Flip it once or twice for uniform cooking. Please remember to cook on medium heat for perfect flat breads. Too much or too less of heat will either char or undercook the bread. Store it in a covered container or box which is lined with a sheet of paper towel. Repeat for the remaining balls of dough.

> **Note:** This layered bread is slightly oily when compared to rotis. Wrap any leftover flat bread in paper towel and place it in a box. If you are going to use it in the next 24 hours, let it stay at room temperature. If not refrigerate it and reheat well on a flat griddle before serving. Enjoy these with vegetables and bean curries. These breads taste best when they are fresh and hot.

Rotis and parathas are the basic Indian breads made at home. Once you understand the process from kneading, to rolling, to cooking, the preparation of breads will become easier, hence less time consuming too. Initially shape, uniform thickness and managing the heat on griddle will be little tricky, after a few mishaps I am sure you will master it. We do learn new lessons every day, so be the bread making too.

Herb bread with cilantro leaves

3. Herb Bread with Cilantro Leaves
(Suitable for Vegans)
SERVING: Makes 8-10

Ingredients

1 cup whole wheat flour
1/3 cup finely chopped cilantro leaves
¼ tsp salt
¼ to ½ tsp black pepper powder
¼ to ½ tsp cumin powder
A dash of turmeric powder
2-3 tsp oil
½ to ¾ cup warm water
½ cup dry flour for rolling
Few spoons of oil for cooking

Method

Combine all the ingredients except for water in a mixing bowl. Using your fingers gently mix the ingredients well. Now add warm water little at a time to knead soft dough. Roll the dough into a ball and keep covered for an hour.

Divide the dough into 8 to 10 balls of equal size and keep them covered. Take one ball of dough, roll it in dry flour and gently roll it between your palms. Place this ball on a board and roll it into a circle of about 8" diameter and uniform thickness. Use dry flour as needed.

Heat a flat griddle and gently transfer the rolled out dough on to it. Reduce the heat to medium and move the bread around gently to avoid burning. Once you see bubbles forming, flip the bread and apply few drops of oil all over the bread. Now flip it again and apply few drops of oil all over the second side. Using a spatula gently press along the edges on both sides of the bread. This ensures uniform cooking. When the bread is ready keep it in a box lined with paper towel.

Repeat the process for the remaining balls of dough. To save time and fuel, roll out a few [4 to 5] and place them on a wax paper. Heat a griddle and cook these rolled out breads one after the other. Serve hot with any vegetable or bean curry and yogurt. Refrigerate any leftovers and reheat well on a griddle before serving.

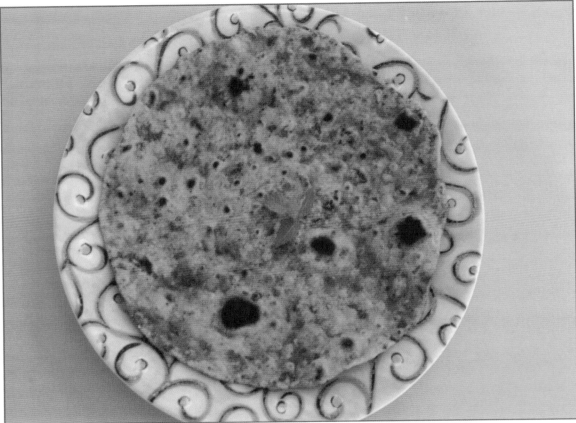

Herb bread with mint leaves

4. Herb Bread with Mint Leaves
(Suitable for Vegans)
SERVING: Makes 8-10

Ingredients

1 cup whole wheat flour
1/3 cup finely chopped mint leaves
½ tsp garam masala powder
¼ to ½ tsp red chilli powder
¼ tsp salt
A dash of turmeric powder
2 tsp oil
½ to ¾ cup warm water
½ cup wheat flour for rolling
Few spoons of oil for cooking

Method

Combine all the ingredients except warm water, in a mixing bowl. Mix well using your fingers. Add warm water little at a time to knead the flour into soft dough. Roll the dough into a ball and keep covered for an hour.

Divide the dough into 8 to 10 balls of equal size. Keep them covered. Take one ball of dough, roll in dry flour and roll well between your palms. Place this ball on a board and roll it out to circle of about 8" diameter and uniform thickness. Use dry flour for rolling as needed. Now the bread is ready to be cooked.

Transfer these rolled out dough to a hot griddle and reduce the heat to medium. Move the flat bread on the griddle using a spatula to avoid the bread from burning or sticking to the griddle. When you see bubbles forming, flip it over and apply few drops of oil evenly all over. Now flip it back and apply few drops of oil all over. Press along the edges using a spatula and repeat it again after flipping it once more. This ensures uniform cooking. Store it in a box lined with paper towel.

Repeat the process for the remaining balls of dough. To save time and fuel, roll out a few and place on a wax paper. Cook them one after the other on a hot griddle.

Serve these with vegetable or bean curries and yogurt. Serve the bread hot. Refrigerate any leftover bread and reheat well on a griddle before serving.

Green split peas bread

5. Green Split Peas Bread
(Suitable for Vegans)
SERVING: Makes 12

Ingredients

1/3 cup green split peas
1 cup [slightly heaped] wheat flour
½ cup warm water [as needed]
½ cup dry flour for rolling

Seasonings

½ tsp coriander powder
¼ to ½ tsp red chilli powder
½ tsp cumin powder
¼ tsp turmeric powder
2 tsp oil
¼ to ½ tsp salt
Little oil for cooking

Method

Cook the green peas with sufficient water to a soft consistency. Pressure cooking is advisable. Place the cooked split peas in a bowl and mash it to a paste. To this add coriander powder, red chilli powder, cumin powder, turmeric powder and salt. Mix well and let it cool. When cooled add the wheat flour and 2 tsp oil and knead a soft dough using warm water as needed. Roll the dough into a ball and keep covered for an hour.

Now divide the dough into 12 balls of same size and keep them covered. Take one ball at a time, roll into dry flour and roll it between your palms with slight pressure. Now you have a flattened ball. Place this flattened ball on a rolling board and roll out into a circle of about 8" in diameter and uniform thickness. Use dry flour as needed.

Heat a griddle well and gently transfer this rolled out dough on to the griddle. Reduce the heat to medium. Gently move it around to avoid sticking and burning. When you see bubbles forming, flip it and apply few drops of oil all over the bread. You will see small bubbles forming again, flip it over and apply few drops oil all over. Using a spatula or a turner gently press along the edges on both sides of the bread. Now the bread is ready, transfer it to a box lined with paper towel and keep covered to maintain freshness.

Note: Cook on medium heat and the water measurement given is only an approximation. Please increase or decrease the quantity of water as required. To save time and fuel, roll out 4 to 6 breads and keep them on wax paper and heat a flat griddle and cook these breads one after the other. Serve hot with vegetable, beans or yogurt. As always store the leftovers in a refrigerator and reheat well on a griddle before serving.

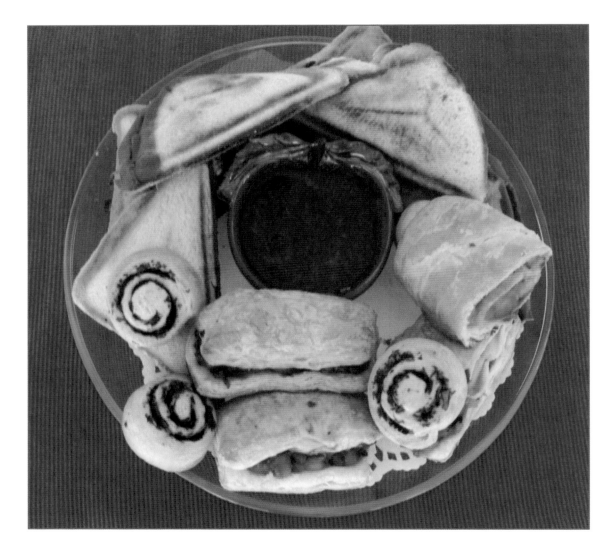

Introduction

This section deals with recipes for miscellaneous items like sandwiches, snacks, and so on. Snacks can be defined as a light meal or refreshment taken between regular meals. Almost all of us indulge in snacking- be it healthy or not. India being highly diverse in cuisine, we have large number of snacks- some light and some are a small meal by itself. Indian snacks are extremely delicious, but can be unhealthy too as many of them are deep fried. Further many are labor intensive and require skilled labor.

Though I prepare a vast variety of snacks-light meals almost every day and fried snacks on special occasions, I am unable to share them as the ingredients are not available in a standard American supermarket. Further the process of preparing them may appear labor intensive and complicated. Fried foods do taste very good but I refrain from preparing them regularly due to health reasons. Further I detest the smell of the oil in the house which is prevalent upon frying.

I really enjoy cooking light meals as my daughters look forward for it when they come home from school very hungry. The light meals are tasty, nutritious and most importantly satisfy their hunger. I have shared few recipes in the following pages keeping in mind my guidelines- simplicity, easily available ingredients and palatable. . Some recipes may appear strange on reading, but please do try on a small scale and if you like it and are comfortable in following the recipe, go ahead and include it in your culinary routine. As always you are the best judge while adding salt. Enjoy your adventures in the kitchen, after all learning is an ongoing process.

Carrot sandwich

1. Carrot Sandwich
(Suitable for Vegans)
Makes 6 triangles with six slices of bread

Ingredients

2 cups grated carrots
¼ cup finely chopped pepper [any color]
¼ cup finely chopped onions
6 slices of bread [any color/any kind]
2 tsp butter or vegetable spread

Seasonings

½ tsp mustard seeds
½ tsp cumin seeds
A dash of turmeric powder
A dash or two [less than ¼ tsp] red chilli powder
2 tsp oil
Salt
2 tsp finely chopped cilantro leaves

Method

Heat oil in a skillet and before it smokes add the mustard seeds and cumin seeds. When the mustard seeds stop spluttering, add turmeric powder and the onions. Sauté the onions on low medium heat till they are half way done. Now add the grated carrots, peppers, red chilli powder, and little salt. Mix well and cook covered for about 5 minutes till carrots soften. Remove from heat. Taste a little to check the salt, add if required. Add cilantro leaves, mix well and let it cool.

Apply butter or vegetable spread lightly on 6 slices of bread. Divide the carrots into 3 equal portions and spread it uniformly on 3 buttered slices of bread. Place on top another slice with buttered side facing the carrots. Place these sandwiches in a preheated sandwich maker and cook till golden brown or well browned.

Serve them hot with soup for lunch or serve them as a light meal anytime. I usually take these on picnics or pack for lunch to school and work. As always refrigerate any leftovers and reheat well on a flat griddle before serving.

Cream of wheat (with spices & vegetables)

3. Cream of Wheat (with Spices & Vegetables)
(Suitable for Vegans)
SERVES 3

Ingredients

- 1 cup cream of wheat
- 1 cup mixed vegetables, cooked [diced carrots, cut green beans, diced potatoes, peas, sweet corn, peppers etc]
- 1 small onion finely chopped
- 2-2 1/2 cups of water

Seasonings

- ¾ tsp mustard seeds
- ¾ tsp cumin seeds
- 1 tsp yellow split peas
- 2" long dried red chilli or jalapeno pepper
- ¼ tsp grated ginger or a dash of ginger powder
- A dash or 2 of turmeric powder
- Salt
- 3-4 tsp oil
- 2 tsp finely chopped cilantro leaves

Method

Roast cream of wheat on medium heat in a skillet for about 4 minutes and transfer it to a bowl. Kindly take care not to brown the cream of wheat. Clean the skillet with a paper towel to reuse it.

Heat oil in the skillet and before it smokes add the mustard seeds, cumin seeds, yellow split peas and the dried chilli. When the mustard seeds stop popping, add the ginger and turmeric powder. Now add the onions and sauté till half done. Now add the cooked mixed vegetables, water, salt and cilantro leaves. Stir well and let it come to a boil. When the water is rapidly boiling, reduce the heat and carefully stir in the cream of wheat while stirring the water with a flat spoon continuously. This will avoid any lumps from forming. After stirring the ingredients of the skillet well, cover it and let cook for about 3 to 4 minutes. Remove from heat and let it stay covered for another 2 to 3 minutes. Discard the chilli.

Add a dash of lime before serving. Serve hot with any kind of chips on the side. This can be a small meal by itself.

> **Note:** This is traditionally a breakfast preparation in southern India. It is made very often as it is easy to prepare and satisfies the hunger well. As always refrigerate any leftover portions and reheat well before serving. If you are using jalapeno pepper, add it after the mustard seeds have stopped crackling. As always discard the jalapeno pepper before serving.

2. Cilantro-Mint Chutney
(Suitable for Vegans)
Makes about 6 oz

Ingredients

2 cups of cilantro leaves lightly packed
½ cup of mint leaves lightly packed
1"long jalapeno pepper
2-3 tsp lime juice
Salt
4-5 oz water

Method

Place cilantro leaves, mint leaves and jalapeno pepper in a blender and blend for about 45 to 60 seconds. Scrape the sides and add water, lime juice and salt. Blend till smooth [about 30-45 seconds]. Store in a bottle, label it and refrigerate it.

Note: The water measurement can be altered to the desired consistency. This chutney can be used as a base for veggie sandwiches, burgers or as a dip for pastry puffs or drizzled over a salad. Stir well with a spoon before using for uniform consistency. It is advisable to make small quantities at a time. Refrigeration is a must.

4. Fried Black-eyed Pea Dumpling
(Suitable for Vegans)
SERVES 3-4

Ingredients

½ cup black eye peas
5 tsp plain bread crumbs [approximately]
¾ tsp cumin powder
¼ tsp red chilli powder
A dash of turmeric powder
Salt
5 tsp finely chopped onions
3 tsp finely chopped cilantro leaves
Oil for frying

Method

Soak black eye peas in water for about 8 to 10 hours. Drain and grind to a coarse paste in a blender or a food processor with minimum water. Transfer to a mixing bowl and keep aside.

Just before frying add bread crumbs, cumin powder, salt, red chilli powder, onions and cilantro leaves. Mix well. Heat sufficient oil in a deep frying pan and check the temperature of the oil by dropping a very small quantity of the paste into the oil. If the paste rises immediately to the top, the oil is ready for frying.

Now carefully drop small lumps or small balls [the size of a cherry] into the oil. You can fry quite a bit at once depending on the size of the deep frying pan. Reduce heat to medium and fry well by turning the dumplings often with a slotted spoon for uniform cooking. When nicely browned remove from oil and drain on a paper towel before transferring to the serving platter. Serve hot.

Note: please ensure that the core of the dumpling is well cooked. Do NOT fry on high heat. The fried dumplings can be stored at room temperature for a day and the leftover paste if any can be refrigerated for maximum of 2 days. You may need to add a little more bread crumbs to the refrigerated paste before frying. However it is advisable to prepare the bean paste as needed. A word of caution- DO NOT USE CANNED BEANS.

5. Fried Split Peas Dumpling
(Suitable for Vegans)
SERVES 3-4

Ingredients

½ cup yellow split peas
1/3 cup green split peas
5 tsp plain bread crumbs
A dash of turmeric powder
A generous dash of red chilli powder
Salt
5 tsp of finely chopped onions
3 tsp of very finely chopped cilantro leaves
Oil for frying

Method

Combine both the split peas and soak it in water for an hour. Drain the water and grind to a coarse paste in a blender or a food processor with minimum water. Transfer this paste to a bowl; just before frying add salt, turmeric powder, red chilli powder, bread crumbs, onions and cilantro leaves. Mix well.

Heat enough oil in a frying pan or skillet. Test the temperature of the oil by dropping a small quantity of paste into the oil. If it rises up immediately the oil is ready for frying. Now drop small lumps or balls into the oil carefully. Reduce the heat to medium and fry well, turning it often with a slotted spoon. When golden brown remove from oil carefully and drain the excess oil on a paper towel. Serve hot with tomato ketchup or mint chutney.

Note: Please add the salt just before frying; if not the excess moisture will make the dumplings soggy. You can replace the cilantro leaves with finely chopped dill leaves or mint leaves. As always refrigerate the paste and you may need to add a couple of spoons of bread crumbs before frying it. The dumplings can stay at room temperature for a day or two. Please follow the normal precautions for frying. Hope you enjoy these dumplings.

6. Oat Meal with Yogurt
(Not Suitable for Vegans)
SERVES 1

Ingredients

- ¼ cup oatmeal [instant or old fashioned]
- ½ cup water [or refer to the instruction chart for water ratio]
- ½ cup PLAIN yogurt, whisked

Seasonings

- ¼ tsp mustard seeds
- ¼ tsp cumin seeds
- ¼" to ½"long dried red chilli
- A pinch or 2 of salt
- 1 tsp oil
- ½ tsp finely chopped cilantro leaves

Method

Heat oil in a saucepan and before it smokes add the mustard seeds, cumin seeds and the dried red chilli. Cover. When the mustard seeds stop crackling, reduce heat to medium and add the oat meal and sauté it for a minute. Add salt and water and stir well. Cook for 2 to 3 minutes till the water is absorbed and the oatmeal is cooked. Transfer it a bowl and let it cool. Discard the red chilli, add yogurt and cilantro leaves, mix well and enjoy a light meal, which is tasty and healthy too.

Microwave method -Place the oatmeal in a microwave safe bowl. Heat oil in a small pan and before it smokes add the mustard seeds, cumin seeds and dried red chilli. Cover. When the mustard seeds stop spluttering, pour the seasoning over the oatmeal. Now add a pinch or two of salt, water and mix well. Microwave for about 90 seconds or till oatmeal is cooked. Cool and mix in yogurt and cilantro leaves and have a light meal.

As always refrigerate any unused portions and DO NOT reheat before serving.

Pinwheels with cilantro leaves

7. Pinwheels with Cilantro Leaves
(Suitable for Vegans)
Makes 16 pinwheels

Ingredients

1 Pillsbury crescent rolls dough
½ cup of very finely chopped cilantro leaves
A dash of salt [optional]
A dash or two of red chilli powder
¼ tsp cumin powder

Method

In a bowl combine cilantro leaves, salt [optional], red chilli powder and cumin powder. Mix well and keep aside. Unroll the crescent roll dough on a flat surface, like a glass cutting board. Cut into 4 rectangles by separating it along the perforated line. Pinch with moist fingers along the diagonal perforated line to seal it. Now you have 4 rectangles instead of 8 triangles.

Divide the cilantro spice mix into 4 equal portions and spread it evenly on four rectangles. Use a rolling pin lightly once over the rectangles to embed the cilantro leaves into the dough. Now carefully roll the rectangle to resemble a small log, with cilantro leaves being inside. Roll widthwise, that is one width edge being inside and the other width edge being outside. Use a wet sharp knife to cut each log into 4 circular slices. Place them on a baking tray and bake at the specified temperature. Be sure to reduce the baking time by a couple of minutes than what is specified. The best way is to keep checking after 7 minutes to avoid burning.

These appetizers are very easy to make and the aroma of cilantro leaves is amazing. Try it out on a small scale and if you like it make more and serve at parties. Your guests will wonder how something can be so easy to make and yet taste so good. I have used Pillsbury crescent dough in the recipe as it is suitable for vegetarians and vegans.

Potato pastry puff

8. Potato Pastry Puff
(Suitable for Vegans)
Makes 9 Puff with 1 sheet

Ingredients

1 sheet of Pepperidge farm pastry puff

1 ½ cups of boiled and mashed potatoes

3 tbsp cooked peas

3tbsp finely chopped onions

Seasonings

1/2 tsp mustard seeds

½ tsp yellow split peas

1"long jalapeno pepper, slit lengthwise

A dash of turmeric powder

Salt

2 tsp oil

tbsp finely chopped cilantro leaves

Method

Heat oil in a small skillet or a pan and before it smokes add the mustard seeds, yellow split peas and turmeric powder. When mustard seeds stop popping add the jalapeno pepper and onions. Sauté for 2-3 minutes. Now add the mashed potatoes, peas, salt and cilantro leaves. Mix well and let it cook for 2-3 minutes. Remove from heat and discard the jalapeno pepper. Cool this filling and then divide into 9 equal portions.

Unroll one sheet of Pepperidge farm pastry puff on a flat board. Cut into 3 pieces lengthwise. Now cut each long piece into 3 equal pieces. Now there are 9 pieces of pastry puffs ready to be stuffed. Place the filling on half of the pastry piece and fold the other half over it. With moist fingers seal the 3 open edges. Now 9 pastry puffs filled with potatoes are ready to be baked.

Bake according to the instructions mentioned on the package regarding temperature and time. It is advisable to keep checking to prevent burning. When done you will notice the sealed edges have separated and this perfectly normal. Serve hot.

Note: These potato puffs are very easy to make and taste delightful. You can alter this basic recipe to suit your taste and preference. As always refrigerate any leftover puffs and reheat on a flat griddle or in a microwave oven before serving.

Potato-peas sandwich

9. Potato-Peas Sandwich
(Suitable for Vegans)
SERVES: 8 triangles with 8 slices of bread

Ingredients

2 cups of mashed potatoes
¼ cup cooked green peas
1/3 cup of onion finely chopped
8 slices of bread [any kind] lightly
  buttered or use vegetable spread

Seasonings

½ tsp mustard seeds
½ tsp cumin seeds
¾ tsp yellow split peas
A dash or 2 of turmeric powder
¼ to ½ tsp red chilli powder
¼ to ½ tsp garam masala
2 tsp oil
Salt
2-3 tsp finely chopped leaves

Method

Place the mashed potatoes in a bowl and add the cooked peas, turmeric powder, garam masala, red chilli powder, salt and the cilantro leaves. Mix well and keep aside. Heat oil in a skillet and before it smokes add the mustard seeds, cumin seeds and yellow split peas. When the mustard seeds stop spluttering, add the onions and sauté it till half way done. Now add the potatoes and sauté for 3 to 4 minutes. Remove from heat and cool it slightly.

Divide this potato filling into 4 equal portions. Spread them uniformly on the 4 buttered slices of bread. Place the remaining slices on top, buttered side facing the potatoes. Place these sandwiches in a preheated sandwich maker and cook till golden brown or well done.

Serve hot with mint chutney or by itself as a light meal or an evening snack. As always refrigerate any unused portions and reheat well on a flat griddle and serve.

Spicy potatoes in crescent roll

10. Spicy Potatoes in Crescent Roll
(Suitable for Vegans)
SERVES: Makes 8 pieces

Ingredients

1 Pillsbury crescent dough roll
1 ½ cup of boiled and mashed potatoes
2 tbsp finely chopped onions

Seasonings

¼ tsp mustard seeds
A generous dash of garam masala powder
A dash of turmeric powder
A generous dash of red chilli powder
2 tsp finely chopped cilantro leaves
Salt
2 tsp oil

Method

Place the boiled potatoes in a mixing bowl. Add the garam masala, turmeric powder, red chilli powder, salt and cilantro leaves. Mix well and keep aside. Heat oil in a skillet and before it smokes add the mustard seeds. When the mustard seeds stop spluttering add the onions and sauté for about 2 minutes. Add the potatoes to the pan and sauté for about 3-4 minutes till the spices are uniformly blended. Remove from heat, keep aside and cool it.

Unroll the Pillsbury crescent dough on a flat surface and cut out the marked rectangles. Pinch with moist fingers along the diagonal cut to seal it. Use a rolling pin to flatten it if required. Now you have 4 rectangles. Divide the potatoes into 4 equal portions and spread it on the rectangular dough leaving 1/2" space on both width ends. Carefully roll it with one width edge inside and the other width edge outside, to resemble a log.

Now you have 4 rolls filled with spicy potatoes, bake it as per the instructions. When done, cut each roll into half and serve it with tomato ketchup or cilantro mint chutney on the side. Serve hot if possible for better taste.

Note: this is very easy to make and well liked by children. As I am not a very comfortable using potato entirely, I add diced carrots, peas, corn, green beans and the like. As always refrigerate any leftovers and reheat well before serving. You can be very creative and can have a variety of fillings like beans, spiced rice etc in the roll and makes it easy for a light meal on the go. Personally I prefer reduced fat crescent dough.

Vegetable pastry puff

11. Vegetable Pastry Puff
(Suitable for Vegans)
SERVES: 9 puffs from 1 sheet

Ingredients

1 sheet Pepperidge farm pastry puff sheet
½ cup finely chopped peppers [any color]
¼ cup or less, finely chopped onions
¼ cup finely chopped carrots
2-3 tbsp green peas
2-3 tsp finely chopped cilantro leaves

Seasonings

½ tsp mustard seeds
A dash of turmeric powder
¼ tsp or less red chilli powder
Salt
2 tsp oil

Method

Heat oil in a small skillet and before it smokes add the mustard seeds. When the mustard seeds stop spluttering add the onions and sauté for 2 minutes. Now add the peppers, carrots, peas and cook covered for about 2 minutes. Add salt, chilli powder, cilantro leaves, mix well and cook covered for about 2 minutes. Remove from heat and keep aside.

Unroll the pastry puff sheet on a lightly floured board or glass cutting board. Cut the sheet into 3 pieces lengthwise. Now cut each piece into 3 pieces of equal size. 9 pieces of pastry dough are ready. Divide the vegetable filling into 9 portions. Place one portion of the filling on lower half of the pastry dough and cover the other half on the filling. With moist fingers seal the 3 open edges. One vegetable filled puff is ready. Repeat the filling process for the remaining 8 pieces of puff dough.

Place on a baking tray and bake at the temperature recommended by the manufacturer. It is advisable to check the bottom of the puff to avoid burning. Serve hot.

Note: As the pastry sheet has little salt, it is advisable to keep it low in the vegetable filling. A grain of less salt is palatable when compared to a grain more. Vegetable puffs are an extremely popular item in Indian bakeries. I had never made it when I was in India, it is here in this country I tried to recreate it with the available ingredients. After one failed attempt I succeeded in mastering it. As these are very easy to make and delicious, these puffs make a delightful appetizer. Please refrigerate any unused puffs and reheat on hot flat griddle or microwave for 30 to 60 seconds. Reheating in a regular oven would be a colossal waste of energy. If the vegetable filling is leftover you can use it to make a vegetable sandwich by placing the filling between 2 slices of bread and placing it in a sandwich maker. It is difficult to make the exact amount of vegetable filling needed.

Vegetable patty

12. Vegetable Patty
(Suitable for Vegans)
<u>MAKES</u> 4 patties

Ingredients

1 cup boiled and mashed potatoes
½ cup mixed vegetables [finely cut carrots, beans, beets, peas, corn] cooked
½ cup boiled and mashed chick peas
1/3 cup plain bread crumbs

Seasonings

½ tsp cumin powder
¼ to ½ tsp red chilli powder
½ tsp curry powder
Salt
Few spoons of oil
2 tsp finely chopped cilantro leaves

Method

Place the potatoes, mixed vegetables and chick peas in a mixing bowl. Add cumin powder, red chilli powder, curry powder, salt and finely chopped cilantro leaves. Mix well using a masher or your fingers ensuring that the spices are evenly and uniformly mixed. Now divide it into 4 balls of equal size.

Heat a flat griddle. Grease your palms slightly and flatten these balls into patties [3-4"in diameter] and roll it into bread crumbs so that it is coated evenly on both sides. Transfer the patties to the hot griddle, drizzle a tsp of oil along the edges and on the patty. After 2-3 minutes turn over, drizzle little oil and let it cook till golden brown. Please see to it that the patties don't burn.

Serve it between hamburger buns with a drizzle of tomato ketchup or cilantro- mint chutney and lettuce leaves, cucumber slices, tomato slices etc. We vegetarians too can enjoy a good burger.

Note: I make it often using leftover vegetables like cauliflower florets, broccoli, lima beans, edamame etc. I reduce the quantity of potatoes and increase the quantity of other vegetables and still it tastes good. I have mentioned a broad outline, please feel free to add or subtract some vegetables and create your own veggie patties. As always refrigerate any leftover patties and reheat on a flat griddle.

Introduction to Desserts

At the end of a meal, however satisfying it was, generally we look forward for desserts. We tend to crave something sweet to end our meal and this craving has given rise to creation of a variety of sweet preparations. The above idea is universally true.

In India though we don't end our daily meal with desserts [partly due to affordability factor and partly due to health factor], we do eat lots and lots of desserts when there is an occasion or opportunity. I personally think this behavior has led to obesity and other health related issues. Every religious occasion demands preparation of a variety of desserts and the number of religious occasions are plenty. Then we have birthdays, death anniversaries and other kinds of celebrations. As mentioned earlier in the book, India has diversity in cuisine due to many reasons. This increases the variety of desserts available along with the European baked desserts [the result of the British rule].

Indian desserts can be classified broadly into 2 categories-easy to make desserts and desserts which need special skills and expertise. The latter category is generally prepared by professional cooks and very experienced women with immense patience. People like me stick to the former category where it is difficult to go wrong. Though I cook and experiment quite a bit, when it comes to desserts I am not very enthusiastic as desserts involve high calorie ingredients. Apart from the lack of specialized skills, I think being diabetic curbs enthusiasm.

However as we do have people over very frequently, I do prepare desserts regularly. Generally Indian desserts have dairy products like milk, butter, clarified butter [ghee]. As India is predominantly Hindu, cow is sacred and holy to us. It is considered auspicious to use dairy products in desserts and these are offered to gods during religious ceremonies. As most of the desserts are dairy based they are not suitable to vegans. Indians are generally not vegans, though the idea of vegan philosophy is slowly making an entry into the mind set of some educated and broad minded people.

In the following pages I have shared few recipes with you that are very simple to make and is fool proof. It is almost impossible to go wrong as it is very easy though unusual. Though I do prepare many more desserts, I have restricted myself to self imposed constraints of easily available ingredients and simple process.

I have used few nuts, dry fruits and spices like cardamom and saffron. Cardamom and saffron are used both in spicy cooking and desserts. I have refrained from using condensed milk, evaporated milk [except in kulfi] as it is inconvenient to open a can, use 2 tablespoons and refrigerate the rest. In case you are making in large quantity, then it is convenient to use a whole can of condensed milk, evaporated milk or even heavy cream. You are the best judge of this. Sugar like salt is tricky to add. Some like it very sweet while others like it mild. I have given a guideline and do adjust it to your preference.

Have a wonderful time in preparing these desserts and I do hope you enjoy them.

1. Carrots in Creamy Milk
(Not Suitable for Vegans)
SERVING: Makes about 12 oz

Ingredients

12 oz milk [preferably whole]
3 whole cardamom pods
Few strands of saffron
1/5 to ¼ cup sugar
¾ cup diced carrots [baby carrots preferred]
2 tsp cashew nut pieces [unsalted]
2 tsp almond pieces

Method

Peel the cardamom pods and powder the tiny black seeds with ¼ tsp sugar with a pestle and mortar. Keep aside. Cook the carrots with just enough water either on stove top or use pressure cooker. Cool and puree it in a blender. Keep aside.

Using very little oil/clarified butter fry the cashew nut pieces, drain and keep aside. In the same pan fry the almond pieces, drain and keep aside along with the cashew nuts.

Combine milk, cardamom powder and saffron strands in a heavy bottom saucepan and bring to boil on medium heat. Reduce the heat and let it simmer for about 10 minutes. Keep stirring often to avoid milk from sticking to the bottom of the pan. Now add the carrot puree, sugar, fried cashew nuts and almond pieces and let it continue to simmer for about 10 minutes. Keep stirring often.

> **Note:** Though this recipe needs little bit of prep work, it is pretty simple to make. I use Bolthouse farm baby carrots and it tastes delightful, but you can use whichever carrots you have on hand. Cardamom seeds or ready to use cardamom powder can be used instead to whole cardamoms. Serve hot or cold depending on the weather. Please keep it refrigerated and reheat if required.

2. Indian Ice Cream [Kulfi]
(Not Suitable for Vegans)
SERVING: Makes a 13X9 Pan

Ingredients

- 12 oz container whipping cream [preferably light]
- 14 oz can of sweetened condensed milk
- 12 oz can of evaporated milk
- Few strands of saffron
- 6-8 cardamom pods
- 4 tbsp green pistachio nut [unsalted]
- 8-10 apricots

Method

Coarsely grind the pistachio nuts in a small food processor and keep aside. Chop the apricots to small pieces and mix it with pistachio nuts and keep aside. Shell the cardamom pods and place the tiny black seeds along with ¼ tsp sugar in a mortar and powder finely with a pestle. Keep aside.

In a large mixing bowl combine whipping cream, condensed milk and evaporated milk. Beat well with a wire whisk or an electric beater for few minutes till frothy. Pour it in a 13 x 9 glass or porcelain pan, add saffron strands, cardamom powder, pistachio nuts and apricots. Mix gently. Cover tightly with plastic wrap and then cover it with foil wrap. Freeze for 24 hours before serving. Cut into squares by dipping a knife in hot water. Refreeze any unused portion immediately.

Note: in India kulfi was our version of ice cream which was set in moulds. It involved lot of time and patience to condense the milk to make it creamy and rich. In USA it is very easy to make it because of ready ingredients and there is no stove cooking involved. You don't have to adhere to the quantity mentioned, you can alter a couple of ounces and it will not make much of a difference in taste. Please do not add saffron and cardamom powder to the mixing bowl as lots of it gets stuck to the bowl leading to wastage. It is worth making it when you have lot of people over especially in warm weather.

3. Oranges in Creamy Milk
(Not Suitable for Vegans)
SERVING: Makes about 12 oz

Ingredients

12 oz milk [preferably whole]

1/5 to ¼ cup sugar

3 whole cardamom pods

Few strands of saffron

8 oz cup of mandarin oranges [in syrup]

Method

Peel the cardamom pods and powder the tiny black seeds with ¼ tsp sugar with a pestle and mortar. Keep aside.

Place milk, saffron strands and cardamom powder in a heavy based saucepan and bring to boil. Reduce the heat and let it simmer. Keep stirring often to avoid milk from sticking to the bottom of the pan. When you see that quantity of milk has reduced and is creamy and thick, add sugar, stir well and let it simmer for a few minutes. Remove from heat and let the milk cool completely.

Drain the syrup from the mandarin oranges and cut them to small pieces. Add these pieces to the milk which has completely cooled down. Refrigerate it for a few hours and serve well chilled.

Note: this is an uncommon dessert in India but I have included it as the availability of easy to use orange sections makes it simple and convenient. If you have time you can add few sections of fresh oranges [peeled, deseeded and without fibers] to this milk as the flavor of fresh oranges is very enticing. You can use a dash or two of ready to use cardamom powder instead of making it. DO NOT HEAT the milk after oranges have been added.

4. Rice Pudding
(Not Suitable for Vegans)
SERVING: Makes about 12-14 oz

Ingredients

1 oz rice [small grained]
20 oz milk [preferably whole]
2-3 cardamom pods
Few strands of saffron
1/3 cup sugar
1 tbsp cashew nut pieces [unsalted]
1 tbsp raisins
1 tbsp slivered almonds
1 tsp clarified ghee/vegetable
shortening

Method

In a heavy bottom pan add a tsp of clarified butter/vegetable shortening and fry the cashew nut pieces to a golden brown, drain and keep aside. In the same pan fry the almond pieces, drain and keep aside with the cashew nut pieces. In the same pan fry the raisins, drain and keep aside with other fried nuts.

Peel the cardamom pods and powder the tiny black seeds along with ¼ tsp sugar using a pestle and mortar. Keep aside.

In the same saucepan place 1 oz of rice and roast it on medium heat till rice turns sparkling white. Now add 12 oz of milk, saffron strands and cardamom powder. Bring it to boil while stirring it regularly. Reduce the heat and let it continue to boil. Add 4 oz milk, sugar and let the rice cook well. When rice has softened add the fried nuts and raisins and 4 oz of milk. Let it boil once more before you remove from heat.

Serve hot in cold weather and well chilled in warm weather. Adding a few cleaned rose petals [red/pink] adds an exotic touch. In India we eat rose petals; hence we have no hesitation in adding them to decorate the edible fares.

> **Note:** once you remove from heat, cool it and refrigerate it. Reheat to serve hot. In case it thickens, boil ½ cup [or as needed] milk and add it to the pudding.

Sweetened cream of wheat

5. Sweetened Cream of Wheat
(Suitable for Vegans)
SERVES 3-4

Ingredients

¾ cup cream of wheat
1/3 to ½ cup sugar
¼ cup finely chopped bananas or pineapple
   pulp
2 cups water
4 tsp oil/clarified butter/vegetable
shortening
3 whole cardamom pods
Few strands of saffron
1 tbsp cashew nut pieces [unsalted]
1 tbsp raisins
Few drops of yellow food color

Method

Peel the cardamom pods and powder the black seeds with ¼ tsp sugar using a pestle and mortar. Keep aside. Measure 2 cups of water in a jug, add saffron strands and yellow food color to it and keep aside. Heat 1 tsp oil/clarified butter/veg. shortening in a skillet and fry the raisins, drain and keep aside. In the same oil/clarified butter/veg. shortening fry cashew nut pieces to a golden brown, drain and keep aside with raisins.

Now heat 3 tsp oil/clarified butter/veg.shortening in the same skillet and add cream of wheat to it. Roast it on low medium heat for about 5 minutes. Now add the cardamom powder and the water [with saffron and color] and stir briskly till it is even in consistency. Let it cook for about 5 minutes. Now add sugar, cashew nuts, raisins, banana or pineapple and mix well. Let it continue to cook for about 5 minutes. Stir often for uniform cooking. Remove from heat and serve hot.

Note: This sweetened cream of wheat is prepared all over India with subtle variations. This is regarded as a simple and quick preparation. Many have it for breakfast [I simply cannot fathom the idea as I am more of a salt and spice person] while others have it for snack or dessert. Most Indians use clarified butter [ghee] instead of oil, but I have mentioned oil as it is convenient and makes it vegan friendly. Generally the quantity of clarified butter used is more than what I have mentioned, you can use more if you like. Instead of making your own cardamom powder, use can use ready to use powder. Adding banana or pineapple eliminates the need for artificial flavoring agents and also lends an exotic touch to this simple fare. This sweetened cream of wheat is generally light yellow in color, please add the food coloring carefully. As always refrigerate leftovers and reheat well before serving. This can stay at room temperature for about 2 days during cold weather, but refrigeration is always advised.

Introduction to Drinks

Water is sacred to all Hindus and if a guest is not offered water, it is considered as an ultimate humiliation to the guest and one of the biggest sins committed by the host. In my culture we cannot deny water even to our worst enemy as this sinful act cannot be justified. In all Indian households a glass of water is placed next to the plate even before the food is served. The warm weather along with the spicy, salty and oily food makes it a necessity to have a glass of water handy. The best drink that complements Indian food is water, preferably a tall glass of cold water.

Water is the most consumed drink in the world and second comes tea. This may sound surprising especially to coffee drinkers, but the fact that tea is consumed more in Asian countries [which are heavily populated] makes it true. Though there are innumerous kinds of tea, I have mentioned only black tea as that is the most consumed by Indians. In India we use the word 'chai' to refer to tea and that is one word that all Indians [a billion plus] will understand in spite of various languages and thousands of dialects. We drink tea anytime of the day irrespective of the weather. In colder weather more tea is consumed especially tea with a hint of spices called 'masala chai'.

Tea unlike coffee is not a bean. It comprises of leaves and sometimes twigs from tea plants. It undergoes a lot of process before it ends up in our kitchen. Most Indians use loose tea leaves instead of tea bags as the flavor is far superior. But from convenience point of view tea bags are preferred. It is just a matter of taste and preference.

Being one of the largest milk producing country in the world and milk being sacred, we consume lot of milk based and yogurt based drinks. Extreme fondness for milk and milk products and the religious importance associated with it, makes it almost impossible for us to be vegans. The heat makes it necessary to include yogurt and buttermilk in our daily diet. Further milk, yogurt, butter, clarified butter are symbols of prosperity and this fact alone makes us consume these products in enormous quantities.

In the following pages I have shared few recipes that are very easy to make. Though these drinks may appear weird at first, do try it as these are not just delightful but also are beneficial to one's health.

1. Spiced Milk
(Not Suitable for Vegans)
MAKES 8 Oz

Ingredients

8 oz milk
2 whole cardamom pods [crushed]
Few strands of saffron
A pinch of nutmeg powder
Sugar/sweetener as needed

Method

Combine milk, cardamom, saffron and nutmeg and bring it boil on low medium heat. Once it starts boiling, reduce heat and let it continue to boil for 5 to 7 minutes. Stir in between to avoid the milk from boiling over. Remove from heat, strain into a cup and add sugar/sweetener if needed. Serve it hot.

Note: Saffron is known to have sedative properties, a cup of this milk before bed time will ensure a good restful sleep. As this milk does not contain artificial ingredients, this milk is beneficial to sleep deprived people.

2. Turmeric-Pepper Milk
(Not Suitable for Vegans)
MAKES 8 Oz

Ingredients

8 oz milk
A dash or two of turmeric powder
¼ tsp black pepper powder
2 tsp honey

Method

Combine milk with turmeric powder and pepper powder and bring it to boil on medium heat. Once it boils, reduce heat and let it continue to boil for another 5-7 minutes. Remove from heat, strain it into a cup and stir in the honey. Drink it hot.

Note: It is very obvious from the ingredients that this milk is not consumed for its taste. This is an age old remedy for relieving the symptoms associated with common cold, sore throat and cough. Though this is not a cure, it does reduce the intensity of discomfort. Turmeric, pepper and honey have been used due to their immense medicinal benefits. The absence of alcohol and artificial ingredients are the plus points of this milk. This homemade remedy has with stood the test of time and has proved itself.

3. Spiced Yogurt [Salt Lassi]
(Not suitable for vegans)
MAKES 8-10 Oz

4. Sweet Yogurt [Sweet Lassi]
(Not suitable for vegans)
MAKES 8-10 Oz

Ingredients

6 oz plain yogurt
1 cup ice cubes
A pinch of ginger powder
A dash of cumin powder
¼ tsp salt [suggested]
2-3 fresh mint leaves

Ingredients

6 oz plain yogurt [preferably from whole milk]
1 oz milk
3-4 tsp sugar
¼ to ½ tsp cardamom powder
1 cup ice cubes

Method

Combine all the ingredients with ONE mint leaf and blend till frothy. Garnish with 1-2 mint leaves and serve well chilled.

Method

Combine all the ingredients in a blender and blend till frothy. Serve it well chilled.

Note: This drink is an excellent accompaniment to Indian food as it helps in digesting all the spices and oil. Generally Indian food served in restaurants is rich and oily and this salt lassi aids in digestion. Anytime one has over eaten or is experiencing discomfort this simple drink can work magic. Once again the natural ingredients can help in alleviating digestion problems. On hot days, a pitcher full of this salt lassi is very much appreciated. The only drawback is many people are not familiar with mixing salt and yogurt and may find it odd. Make a small glass and if you like it make more and this can keep you cool in summer.

Note: Please use only plain yogurt. This natural drink is a wonderful cooling agent for the body. Yogurt calms the digestive system and the absence of artificial chemicals makes this simple drink very desirable.

5. Mango Milk Shake
(Not suitable for vegans)
MAKES 10 Oz

Ingredients

6 oz milk

1 ripe mango, cut into small pieces

4 tsp sugar

¼ to ½ tsp cardamom powder

Few strands of saffron

1 cup ice cubes

Method

Cut the cheeks of the ripe mango and using a steel serving spoon scoop out the fruit. Cut the scooped fruit into pieces. Using a sharp knife cut out as much fruit as possible from the seed/stone. Discard the peel.

Combine all the ingredients in a blender and blend till smooth. Serve this exotic drink chilled.

Note: Instead of using 6 oz milk you can use 6 oz plain yogurt and 1 oz milk and the same other ingredients and make mango lassi. Serve well chilled.

6. Masala Chai
(Not suitable for vegans)
MAKES 8 Oz

Ingredients

7 oz water

1 ½ -2 oz milk

1 tsp [slightly heaped] black tea leaves

¼ tsp fresh grated ginger

1-2 whole cardamom pods [crushed]

Sugar/sweetener as needed [generally a tsp]

Method

Place water, grated ginger and cardamom in a saucepan and let it come to a rolling boil. Reduce heat, add tea leaves, stir once and let it boil for a minute. Now add the milk and let it boil once. Remove from heat and strain into a cup/mug using a tea strainer. Add sugar or sweetener if required and relax with a cup of masala chai especially on cold days.

Note: This tea is very beneficial to the body especially during cold weather or if you are suffering from symptoms of a common cold or sore throat.

7. Tea
(Not suitable for vegans)
<u>MAKES 8 Oz</u>

Ingredients

7 oz water
1-2 oz milk
1 tsp [slightly heaped] black tea leaves
Sugar to taste [generally 1 tsp]

Method

Place water in a saucepan and bring it to boil. Add the tea leaves, reduce the heat, and stir once with a spoon. After a minute add milk and let it come to boil just once. Remove from heat and strain it into a cup/mug using a tea strainer. Add sugar or sweetener as required and enjoy a cup of stimulating Indian tea.

> **Note:** in India we generally boil the milk and then refrigerate it and use all day for tea, coffee etc. As in this country we do not have boiled milk ready on hand, I have suggested letting the milk boil while preparing tea. This makes the tea taste better and stays hot for a longer time.

Here is how to cut a ripe Mango

Introduction to Fruits

India being diverse in topography and geographical conditions makes it possible for us to enjoy both tropical and temperate fruits in abundance. Though we have a variety of tropical fruits, mango is considered as 'the king' of the fruits. When I was growing up we had a massive mango tree and it was a delight in spring time to watch it sprout new tender leaves [which were very aromatic], flowers, and then the fruit. Raw mangoes are green in color, hard and sour, this sourness makes the raw mangoes very much desired. Raw mangoes are used in variety of pickles [with lot of spices and oil], chutneys, sweet and sour preserves, mango rice, dips, so on and so forth.

Come summer and markets are flooded with ripe mangoes [lot of varieties]. The use of ripe mangoes is slightly limited when compared to the uses of raw mango. Ripe mangoes are made into juice, pulp, jam and fruit leather. But the best way to enjoy a ripe mango is to cut it into pieces and eat it simply, without any process or much ado.

Ripe mangoes are multi hued- predominantly yellow with hints of orange, red and green.

Many of my non Indian friends have asked me as to 'how to eat a mango?' The easy and neat way is as follows; wash the mango well and place it on a cutting board. Cut the cheeks of the mango with a sharp knife, with a big metal spoon scoop out the fruit, working along the edges. Throw out the peel and cut the scooped fruit into small pieces. Remove the peel from the stone/seed which is in the centre of the mango. Cut away as much fruit as possible and discard the stone/seed. Serve in a bowl with a small fork.

You can use these pieces in a milk shake or fruit salad or eat it by itself. Always refrigerate the cut mango pieces.

A hint- if you prepare a fruit salad with pieces of watermelon, pineapple, guava and orange sections, add a pinch of cumin powder, a pinch of pepper powder and a dash of salt just before serving. A slight hint of spices makes this salad exotic. Serve chilled.

Fruity Relish

Those who crave for something different yet palatable do try this simple recipe which needs no cooking. This relish is great with corn chips and spices up the appetizers.

In a bowl combine 2 tbsp finely chopped onions, 1/4 cup diced tomatoes, ¼ cup pieces of peach, ½ cup ripe mango pieces, ¼ cup finely chopped pineapple pieces, 3 tsp finely chopped cilantro leaves. Add ½ tsp cumin powder and ¼ to ½ tsp red chilli powder, mix well with a light hand and chill. Before serving add salt and 2 tsp lemon juice. Enjoy the various tastes like sweet, sour and spicy in one dish.

Fruity relish

Fruits